Father Figure

Also by Jordan Shapiro

The New Childhood: Raising Kids to
Thrive in a Connected World

Father Figure

HOW TO BE A

DAD

JORDAN SHAPIRO

Little, Brown Spark
New York   Boston   London

Little, Brown Spark
Hachette Book Group
1290 Avenue of the Americas, New York, NY 10104
littlebrownspark.com

First Edition: May 2021

Little Brown Spark is an imprint of Little, Brown and Company, a division of Hachette Book Group, Inc. The Little, Brown Spark name and logo are trademarks of Hachette Book Group, Inc.

The publisher is not responsible for websites (or their content) that are not owned by the publisher.

The Hachette Speakers Bureau provides a wide range of authors for speaking events. To find out more, go to hachettespeakersbureau.com or call (866) 376-6591.

ISBN 978-0-316-45996-9
Library of Congress Control Number: 2021934333

Printing 1, 2021

LSC-C

Printed in the United States of America

Dedicated to Angie Murimirwa, Lydia Wilbard, Lucy Lake, and all the members of the CAMFED Association; you taught me that there's nothing idealistic or naïve about believing in the restorative power of participatory and emergent leadership.

CONTENTS

He was not wrong, of course, but he joined all the "woke" white men who set their privilege outside themselves — as in, I know better than to be ignorant or defensive about my status in our world. Never mind that that capacity to set himself outside the pattern of white male dominance is the privilege. There's no outrunning the kingdom, the power, and the glory.

—Claudia Rankine

Father Figure

INTRODUCTION

THE DAD'S DILEMMA

MONDAY, JANUARY 7, 2019, 7:35 A.M.*:* I opened my eyes in a Nashville hotel room. I was tired from a little too much hot chicken and country music the night before. I wanted to go back to sleep, but my phone kept vibrating against the bedside table. Text messages from my mother: *Was happy to see your book in the Wall Street Journal. But I didn't like the review. It was mean.* I read Mom's words aloud to my partner, Amanda, who was lying in bed next to me, scrolling through her own morning notifications. She had a similar message from her sister about the same article.

My book, *The New Childhood: Raising Kids to Thrive in a Connected World*, had been published the previous week and I was in Nashville to promote it. We made a whole weekend of it, traveling with friends from Denmark who wanted to see Music City, USA, before their work visas expired. We planned to meet the Danes for biscuits, fried chicken, and sausage gravy at Monell's — undoubtedly the best breakfast in America — in a couple of hours, but I needed to see that newspaper now!

Amanda and I got dressed quickly and took the elevator down to the lobby. The Noelle hotel is a perfect example of 1930s Art Deco architecture, with super-high ceilings, arched windows, polished brass fixtures, and shiny pink Tennessee marble walls. It's located just off Printer's Alley, a historic district that was once home to two newspapers, ten print shops, and thirteen publishers — a good place to stay if you're a geeky writer, preoccupied with history. We found the *Wall Street Journal* near the espresso machine, on the hipster coffee counter, and sat down to read it on one of the oversize blue sofas.

At first, I was thrilled when we flipped to the opinion page and I saw my book's cover, pictured in full color on the top left corner. This is the kind of placement authors long for. But then I read the review. The first sentence said, "When Jordan Shapiro and his wife separated several years ago, their sons were 4 and 6 years old." The author led with my divorce and in the following paragraphs she did everything she could to cast me in the role of the overpermissive, too-cool, deadbeat dad. Trashing my pro–video game argument for more family screen time, she wrote, "He was all too happy to indulge his sons, even if their mother, apparently, was not." For the record, neither my kids nor my ex-wife understands where this journalist got the idea that we have a tense coparenting relationship. We don't, but that's not the point. The real issue is the implication that a divorced dad can't know much about parenting. My doctorate degree in depth psychology, as well as all my credentials as a recognized expert in child development and education were rendered completely irrelevant for this writer. All because she believed that a good father should be the head of a traditional heterosexual household.

I'm not Ward Cleaver (*Leave It to Beaver*), Phil Dunphy (*Modern Family*), or Howard Cunningham (*Happy Days*). I'm not even Mike Brady (*The Brady Bunch*). I'm a single dad, sharing half-time custody of my sons. Apparently, a lot of people think I live in some sort of velvet-upholstered playboy bachelor pad, where lounge music blasts from audiophile loudspeakers and children have no boundaries. As I traveled the United States, promoting a parenting book, I discovered that many folks immediately jumped to the conclusion that I can't possibly know what's in my own children's best interest because I'm divorced. This prejudice felt especially hurtful to me. I had spent years writing articles, op-eds, and a book full of personal stories about my experience being a dad. Fatherhood was at the core of my identity. My relationship with my children not only defined my career, but also shaped my sense of self-worth. First and foremost, I saw myself as a father figure. It had never occurred to me that being divorced might preemptively exclude me from fitting in to the prevalent cultural understanding of what it means to be a good father.

Over the course of the next year, the book received mostly glowing reviews, but the divorced-dad stigma was always present. I started to see it everywhere I looked: throughout pop culture, and on both sides of the partisan political spectrum. For example, in April 2019 Michelle Obama was speaking in London when she said, "Sometimes you spend the weekends with divorced dad and that feels like it's fun, but then you get sick." The former first lady was criticizing Donald Trump. "That's what America's going through. We're kind of living with divorced dad right now." I was shocked that she would so brazenly undermine the millions of unmarried fathers who are trying to do what's best for their children.

According to the Pew Research Center, "the share of unmarried parents who are fathers has more than doubled over the past 50 years. Now, 29% of all unmarried parents who reside with their children are fathers, compared with just 12% in 1968." And research about how the gender of solo parents impacts children remains inconclusive, maybe because it's too difficult to establish comprehensive criteria. For example, when it comes to academic performance, children of solo fathers tend to get better grades and have higher high-school graduation rates, while solo moms tend to adhere to more so-called traditional routines, such as family dinner. One set of outcomes is not necessarily better than the other. What researchers can say for sure is that children are most likely to thrive in households with loving, supportive, dedicated parents — single or coupled; male, female, or gender nonconforming. There's no evidence to suggest that dysfunctional female-headed households are better than dysfunctional male-headed households, nor that gender identity or marital status has any correlation with dysfunction. Nevertheless, stigmas persist because Americans take their "family values" so seriously. According to historian Stephanie Coontz, Teddy Roosevelt was the first president who warned American citizens that "the nation's future rested on 'the right kind of home life.'" Almost a century later, Ronald Reagan added his voice to a slew of others, saying that "strong families are the foundation of society."[1] But what is the right kind of home life? What is a strong family? It's not clear.

As I'll explain in this book, the nuclear family, as we've come to imagine it, with certain gendered expectations for mothers and fathers, is neither essential nor traditional. It's just a product of the Industrial Age. Today, the dominant labor, economic, and gender norms are all in transition, yet most of our assumptions about family values — which were established to reinforce the worldview of a bygone technological era — remain the same. We've been stubborn about updating our understanding of family life even though we all know that it is unrealistic to expect that so much about our world could change without completely disrupting everything else. Family will change. It's inevitable. In fact, it's already changing, but most parents are unprepared to deal with it. They're wedded to old beliefs that no longer provide an adequate foundation on which to build meaningful identity narratives. The kids will most likely be fine, but their parents are in for a rude awakening.

This book is specifically for fathers and about fatherhood. It considers the way popular images and assumptions about father figures are entwined with problematic attitudes around gender, sex, power, aggression, heteronormativity, and authority. Bad ideas about dads are deeply embedded in our taken-for-granted beliefs about child development, mature adulthood, and professional success. They even shape our primary understanding of individual psychology. These ideas may have been useful once, but in the current world they cause more harm than good, so in the following pages I'll identify some of those troublesome narratives about fatherhood. I'll also offer aspirational images of a new kind of father figure — one that's less paternal, less dominant, and not necessarily masculine.

This book can also be seen as a first-aid kit for dads who feel like they've been wounded as they tried to reconcile their expectations for parenthood, and their identities as mature men, with a culture that's actively shedding its old patriarchal inclinations. Many men today find themselves paralyzed as they confront conflicting messages. To go all in on feminism seems to betray the customary good-dad story. To go all in on the prevailing good-dad story undoubtedly betrays feminism. Even those who make valiant efforts to mediate these tensions often fail to recognize how their unconscious commitment to patriarchal narratives reinforces systemic inequality. They feel whiplashed when their good intentions backfire, so I'll show dads how they can be better attuned to the current cultural ethos. Fathers can play a different kind of caretaking role in their children's lives, and they can leverage a different kind of parental identity narrative, fortifying a stronger sense of self. They can be feminist dads.

What is a feminist dad? Let's start by defining feminism. I prefer the definition with which bell hooks — acclaimed author, theorist, professor, and social activist — began her book, *Feminism Is for Everybody: Passionate Politics*: "Simply put, feminism is a movement to end sexism, sexist exploitation, and oppression."[2] I like how straightforward this statement is — not complicated, scary, or unwelcoming. It also doesn't suggest a battle between men and women. Feminism begins with a forceful criticism of the binary gender–based hierarchy that allocates male privilege, permits dominance and violence, and promotes misogyny and homophobia. However, hooks's definition is open-ended enough to leave room for us to acknowledge that patriarchy can also hurt men. It strips them of certain rights, challenges their self-esteem, and pressures them to adopt sexist identity narratives. Author Chimamanda Ngozi Adichie put it nicely, "Masculinity is a hard, small cage, and we put boys inside this cage."[3] Women are not the only victims of sexism, and men are not the sole perpetrators. Patriarchy is a problem for everyone, whether you're a subjugate or a beneficiary.

bell hooks's work was my first introduction to serious feminist thought. After years of seeing men become defensive at the mere mention of the f-word, hooks offered me an entryway into feminism. She showed me how to take responsibility for my actions without having to feel like a super-villain. When I began to write this book, I pulled my dog-eared and heavily highlighted copy of *Feminist Theory: From Margin to Center* off my bookshelf and reread it. One line stood out immediately: "Feminism is neither a lifestyle nor a ready-made identity or role one can step into."[4] I wrote it on a Post-it Note and attached it to the top of my computer monitor. As a cisgendered man[5] writing a book about feminism, I knew I had to be sure that I wasn't ever virtue signaling — wearing a feminist costume to earn progressive accolades. (Note: *Cis-* is a Latin prefix meaning "on this side of," as opposed to *trans-*, meaning "across." A cisgendered individual's identity corresponds with the sex assigned at birth.) hooks's comment reminded me that, although I was exploring the fatherhood identity, being a "feminist dad" could not be reduced to a two-dimensional part that's played by folks who identify as men. You may indeed see yourself as a father figure the moment you become responsible for a child, but being a feminist dad will always be an ongoing, iterative practice. Despite the subtitle of this book, it's actually not something you are; it's something you do. It's not about being, but rather becoming. You can always go further — there are always more stereotypes to challenge, additional inequities that need attention. Maybe you start by eschewing the common division of household duties. Who cooks in the kitchen? Who *mans* the barbecue grill?[6] Maybe you're careful not to buy products that capitalize on sexism by advertising with slogans such as "Choosy Moms Choose Jif," as if dads aren't discerning when it comes to nutrition and peanut butter sandwiches.[7] Perhaps you avoid the blue/pink, trucks/dolls, sports/glamour dichotomy that's omnipresent in newborn fashion, nursery design, and new-baby greeting cards. Perhaps you'll choose to raise your child as gender neutral, using they/them pronouns to protect them from the asphyxiating grip of patriarchal expectations and stereotypes. No matter where you are on the continuum, feminism is just a framework that informs the actions you take, the decisions you make, and the attitudes you adopt. It always requires self-reflection, evaluation, and constant reinvention.

So, how do you do it? If you're looking for a book full of effortless advice on how to raise confident girls and caring boys, this is not the one. Certainly, I think it's urgent that dads learn how to compliment their daughters in ways that counteract the persistent patriarchal messaging about women's inferiority; but this is not a phrasebook designed to teach you what to say to the young women in your life. Likewise, it's vital that dads teach their boys how to relate to girls in ways that counteract the common misogynistic view of sex, consent, privilege, and complacency, but don't expect a list of talking points to thwart rape culture, or to address your teenager's obsessive porn-watching habit. This is not a parenting book — at least it doesn't fit the genre in familiar ways. Instead, it's more like a guide to self-intervention. It urges fathers to change their mindsets, temperaments, and dispositions. It aims to help dads acknowledge the things they do — ordinary, commonplace, run-of-the-mill things — that replicate problematic attitudes and strengthen oppressive systems.

Of course, you won't be able to eradicate a lifetime's worth of sexist, patriarchal thought patterns by reading this one book. Why? Because feminism is not a fixed solution to a static problem. Instead, it's a variable tool that gives you the ability to make intentional anti-sexist and gender-sensitive choices in dynamic, ever-changing contexts. I'll show you how to use it, and in the process I'll offer an aspirational image of a new

kind of father figure, a model for dads who are desperately trying to navigate their way through a world of changing narratives. Please remember, feminist dad is not an identity. Paradoxically,
you still can, and should, try to become one.

My process of becoming a feminist dad includes four foundational principles:

1. You'll actively cultivate *critical consciousness*. This means
   you're willing to engage critiques of what bell hooks often
   calls "imperialist white-supremacist capitalist patriarchy." I
   know it sounds extreme, maybe more radical and subversive than you expected when you picked up this book. Be
   open-minded. hooks says the phrase simply describes "the
   interlocking political systems that are at the foundation of
   our nation's politics."[8] She can be considered one of the first
   intersectional theorists, acknowledging that it's disingenu-
   ous to talk about gender inequality without also talking
   about sexuality, race, and socioeconomic status. A feminist
   dad acknowledges this fact. He tries to view the world
   through a critical, intersectional lens, and aims to identify,
   interrogate, and then reframe problematic and unjust narratives. He's also critical of the financial, economic, political, technological, and legal structures that are designed to
   steer us away from questioning patriarchal thinking. A
   feminist dad takes this stance even when the self-referential
   gaze burns because his beloved privileges are at stake —
   when he's forced to acknowledge things he'd rather not.

2. You'll practice *responsive fathering*. This means you're adaptable, reflexive, and open to diverse and multifaceted perspectives. You're dedicated to counteracting *narcissistic patriarchal authority*, which is the term I use in part two of this book to describe the taken-for-granted assumption that cisgendered men — especially fathers — are entitled to define and/or be the protagonists of the narrative reality that shapes everyone else's experiences. The prioritization of a dad's life is often cemented into our institutions. For example, medical research still approaches adult male anatomy as the default. It's not just biology; I see the same pattern in my own professional endeavors. The western academic literary canon remains male-centric, and our psychological theories are still inexplicably dependent on gendered myths about patrilineage.

3. You'll be committed to raising your children in an environment devoid of what I call *locker-room gender essentialism* in part three of this book. This means you're willing to shed the narratives of biological determinism and replace them with anti-sexist rhetoric and actions. "Biology is an interesting and fascinating subject," Chimamanda Ngozi Adichie wrote in her book offering advice on raising a feminist daughter, but "never accept it as justification for any social norm. Because social norms are created by human beings, and there is no social norm that cannot be changed."[9] A feminist dad knows this is true. He also recognizes how easy it is for a parent's behavior to inadvertently reinforce

the presumption that oppressive gender conventions are grounded in natural law. In addition, he knows that sexism is ubiquitous, so he goes out of his way to create alternatives for his children to witness.

4. You'll practice rigorous inclusivity. In the simplest terms, this means you're committed to parenting in ways that challenge traditional sexist stereotypes and gender binaries. In other words, feminist dad doesn't ask, how do I prepare my children for the tough realities of a gendered world? Instead, he acknowledges that it's his duty to raise people who are prepared to challenge all forms of sexism, misogyny, injustice, and oppression. A father figure owes it to the rest of humankind to cultivate a nonviolent and nondominant demeanor, modeling for his children an attitude of acceptance and an appreciation for diversity. A feminist dad extends his commitment to equality beyond just cisgender prejudices, fighting to create a safer world for transgender, nonbinary, and other gender-nonconforming individuals, too. In fact, he rejects all forms of discrimination, exploitation, indignity, and coercion. He knows that consent is a prerequisite not only for sex, but also for education, work, religion, spirituality, psychology, policy, and play.

I recognize that right now these four principles may seem somewhat vague and confusing. Maybe you're ready to argue against a few of them, but I implore you, please hold tight. The rest of this book is dedicated to making them clear and irrefutable. Unfortunately, there's no quick and easy way to do it.

I will revisit the four principles in detail in the final section. Even if you skip ahead, you won't find concise or simple explanations for any one of these ideas. They overlap and blend together. Likewise, becoming a feminist dad requires that all four principles be at play, all at once, all the time, so, mirroring this, I've written the book in an interdisciplinary fashion.

From the outset, I want to be clear about one thing. I'm not holding myself up as some sort of luminary feminist dad. I don't abide by all four principles all the time. I certainly try my best, but I also make a lot of mistakes. Many nights, when I'm lying in bed before falling asleep, the first thing I feel is regret. I think of all the problematic interactions I've had with my kids during the day. I replay them in my mind, reviewing my choices, condemning my errors. Then I resolve to be a better parent — and a better feminist dad — tomorrow. That's why this book is full of anecdotes describing my blunders. While I filled *The New Childhood* with positive, inspirational stories about family screen time and joint media engagement, this book is different. I want to show readers how I've learned to practice recognizing and reconsidering the unconscious and regrettable ways that I participate in sexist, patriarchal, binary, misogynistic systems and structures. I hope you can learn to do the same.

I'll be honest. At first, becoming a feminist dad hurts. A lot. But in the long run, it's liberating.

PART ONE

IN THE NAME OF THE FATHER

THURSDAY, 6:15 A.M.: I'm gazing out the windows of our twelfth-floor, three-bedroom apartment. Dawn illuminates the Philadelphia skyline and I snap a photo for Instagram. *#RosyFingers #HomericEpithets #Philly*

It's time to start hollering at my kids. Get out of bed! Brush your teeth! Put your shoes on! Pack your lunches! I flip on their bedroom lamps — bright, drastic, and severe. Light dissolves the shadows and my kids squeeze their eyes shut, resisting illumination like the prisoners freed from Plato's cave. I march down the hallway toward the kitchen.

I need coffee, double espresso, while I'm listening to the news.

Twenty minutes later: I'm caffeinated. I've reviewed the lecture on ancient Greece and the origins of philosophy that I'll deliver to Temple University students later this morning, but my kids are still under the covers.

"Why do you think I pay for your smartphones?" I shout, "Just for YouTube? Learn how to set an alarm or I'm turning off your data plan." Ugh! It's the worst timbre of my own father's voice and it's coming out of *my* mouth — involuntary, bitter, and rancid like vomit.

"Do you really think I want to start my day by screaming?" I ask disingenuously, escalating my irrational anger as if it's their fault. Of course, it's not. I'm just frustrated because I'm hearing the soundscape of my own adolescence and I don't like being trapped in a cyclical algorithm, an intergenerational recipe for household drama. I don't like the tragedy of mindlessly performing a role, reciting a script — especially one that I didn't write. I button up a blue oxford, thread my belt through its loops, and glance at the mirror to see whether this shirt reveals my expanding, middle-aged belly. It does. I decide to wear a darker color, something more slimming.

Now I'm combing my beard and thinking about Ram Dass, spiritual teacher and hippie guru to my father's generation. He once said, "If you think you're enlightened, go spend a week with your family." He was talking about the way old patterns trigger poorly considered reactions and emotional responses. We all know it's true. Family drama can feel inescapable, enclosed and recurring like a player-piano roll. That's the real reason why this morning routine hits me so hard. It's disempowering. It's evidence of my own lack of autonomy. My anger toward my children swells in proportion to my disappointment with myself. I hear the dissonance of my own emotional vulnerability and I do exactly what I assume my father — and so many men before him — always did. I flex my muscles, show off what little authority I can muster.

If I can't control my own actions, you'd goddamn better believe that I'm going to try to control yours!

I bark until my throat is sore. I shepherd my boys toward that awkward moment when we all stand at the front door — coats on, backpacks slung across our shoulders, nudging our fingers into our gloves. We're ready to head out on the day's journey, but for some reason we stop to take a breath before undoing the dead bolt. It's almost like we're — all three of us — acknowledging that we've been acting out some sort of primordial improvisational drama.

We pause, as if to give an imaginary audience a chance to applaud, and then we exit stage right.

Act Like a Man

People are always performing. Like actors, we embody roles and characters. You've probably heard the overplayed line from Shakespeare's *As You Like It*: "All the world's a stage. And all the men and women merely players." More recently, Kurt Vonnegut opened his 1962 novel *Mother Night* with the sentence, "We are what we pretend to be."[1] These words are much deeper than just poetic sentiment.

Consider the word *person*. It comes from the classical Latin *persona*, which once referred to the mask a player wore, not only in a dramatic role but also during ritual. Think about the powdered wigs that Britain's barristers wear. They are clear residual manifestations of those ancient ceremonial *persona* masks. Likewise, a bride's white wedding gown, a priest's collar, and a professional athlete's team uniform — these are all modern cases of *persona* being implemented in the traditional sense, as costumes and vestments to accompany a ritual performance. There are many more subtle examples: a dark pinstriped business suit, perfectly polished cap-toed dress shoes, the smooth synthetic sheen of an Under Armour golf shirt. And it's not just our clothing. We also tailor our vocabularies. Think of the way sitcoms like *The Office* or *Silicon Valley* mock buzzwords and acronyms, the silly scripts that folks use in corporate or start-up settings. You've got to know the language if you want to fit in and succeed! Combine that with learned etiquette and situation-specific routines or behaviors. Soon, you get a sense of the intricate play-acting that constitutes your social reality.

The famous Swiss psychologist Carl G. Jung used the term *persona* to designate an individual's outward-facing attitude.[2] He described it as "a kind of mask, designed on the one hand to make a definite impression upon others, and, on the other, to conceal the true nature of the individual."[3] Jung knew that we all metaphorically dress in uniforms and costumes designed to communicate belonging and status, to show that we are the rightful players of the everyday parts we intend to enact. For me, this give-and-take improv game becomes readily apparent when I arrive home from work at the end of the day. As I slide my arms into a cardigan sweater, I think of Mister Rogers. I imagine the huge pedestal TV cameras and bright Fresnel lamps that sat just beyond the proscenium of his make-believe living room. I step into my fuzzy, warm house slippers and offer my kids a healthy after-school snack. Then, I sternly suggest that they focus on their homework before they start playing video games. I want to encourage good habits. I want to teach them to prioritize their obligations responsibly. But as I'm slicing apple wedges and carrying them to the table, I wonder if I'm just acting like a father, adopting a dad's persona. Am I simply trying to play the part in the only way I've ever seen it played? That's what the famous sociologist Erving Goffman would say. He described human mental life as the product, not the cause, of an ongoing social performance. His most famous book, *The Presentation of the Self in Everyday Life*, was published in 1956, and it's now one of the most cited social science books of all time.[4] Theater was the book's core metaphor.

The self, Goffman explained, "is not an organic thing that has a specific location, whose fundamental fate is to be born, to mature, and to die; it is a dramatic effect arising diffusely from a scene that is presented, and the characteristic issue, the crucial concern, is whether it will be credited or discredited."[5] What he means is that the self, as we know it, is created in response to its social context. My identity is not a product of nature—at least not in the sense that I have a true, inner, authentic self, or a unique biologically predetermined disposition. Rather, for Goffman, the individual self is just the effect, not the cause.[6] We discover who we are as we stage-manage our performances, receiving feedback from our audiences (who are also our fellow actors). The process of self-discovery is the same as learning social behavior. It's like a dress rehearsal: We take the role as it's written, and we try new things — always seeking a standing ovation. To paraphrase superstar singer-songwriter Taylor Swift: We become the people they want us to be.[7]

But remember, nobody goes to the theater without prede-termined expectations, least of all the actors, so, in real life, where do those expectations come from? How do we get our scripts? Who writes them? How do I know what it means to be a father, to feel like a dad? Did it all come from my child-hood experiences? Are we molded for the parental roles we'll eventually play just by watching our parents? Or are there some things about the human family that are absolute and innate? Is there some deep, psychological patterning, the way Jung imagined the archetypes of the collective unconscious? Are we born with hardwired, essential truths already in place? Fixed neurological structures shaped by eons of evolutionary adaptation? Are the stage directions of fatherhood written into our DNA?

Certainly, some research suggests that men undergo biolog-ical changes when they're expecting children. Testosterone lev-els dip, prolactin and cortisol levels rise.[8] There also seems to be increased activation in areas of the brain linked with attach-ment and nurturing.[9] And those fathers who undergo the greatest physical fluctuations tend to take more responsibility for infant caretaking once the baby's born. Does that indicate a causal connection? Does that mean the motivation to be an involved dad is biologically determined? Not necessarily.

Some researchers, looking more closely at men's prenatal physical changes, note that they don't correlate with the number of days remaining until birth. Instead, men's bodies seem to mirror similar hormonal shifts happening to the mother.[10] So it's nearly impossible to trace the line of causality with any real certainty. In other words, nobody knows for sure whether it happens because of the baby or the spouse, the child's gestation or the mother's pregnancy. The father's biological changes could be purely psychosomatic — an unconsciously triggered sympathetic expression of domestic partnership, the body's way of adopting a husband's persona.

Many psychologists have written about cases in which expectant fathers experience weight gain, nausea, loss of appetite, and other symptoms ordinarily associated with women and pregnancy. Experts call this "Couvade syndrome." It's a name derived from the Old French verb *couver*, which can mean both "cowardly inactivity" and "to sit on" — to hatch like a bird on an egg.[11] The term was coined in the mid-nineteenth century by anthropologists who studied so-called primitive cultures. Many of these researchers identified examples of ritualized customs in which the father feels (or at least pretends to feel) the mother's labor pains.[12] It may sound crazy, but the great Sir James Frazer, a folklorist famous for his influential book *The Golden Bough* (1890), attributed Couvade to the belief in "sympathetic magic," explaining that the lack of tangible, measurable, and efficient causality is irrelevant because "the idea that persons and things act on each other at a distance" is commonplace among indigenous cultures.[13]

Modern medicine, early anthropology, psychology, and comparative mythology all have different explanations for what appears to be a common phenomenon associated with pre-fatherhood. They all seem to agree that a man's prenatal transformation is somehow related to the way he thought about the gendered division of postpartum labor even before the pregnancy began. Which hints at more of the same questions: Where do *those* ideas come from? Are men's and women's child-rearing roles innate, fixed, universal? Is there a natural difference between the psychology of how men and women, or mothers and fathers, relate to their children? What happens with same-sex couples? Does one partner act like a mom, the other a dad? If so, it's probably by choice, influenced by cultural expectations. Ultimately, it doesn't seem to have much impact on the children's developmental outcomes. Research has consistently shown that there are no differences that can be attributed solely to the sexuality, gender, or biological sex of the parents.[14] Those who disagree with this scientific consensus[15] tend to base their opinions on outdated assumptions about maternal or paternal influence. They might say something like, "A boy needs a father to teach him how to be a man!" But it's not true.

As this book will show, there's nothing solid at the foundation of gender-specific parenting roles. The way we think about fatherhood is merely the result of arbitrary cultural expectations that are promoted and maintained by religious sermons, television commercials, and bad science — ideas that are reinforced through everyday interactions. It's socialization. We teach men how to play the part of "Dad." We send signals encouraging them to do it the way most people expect to see it done. I know this is true because I've experienced it firsthand.

Be the Breadwinner

When my oldest son was born, I celebrated with a shot of bourbon. At home that first week, I held him in my arms while listening to the entire catalog of Beatles songs in chronological order. We started with "I Saw Her Standing There" on *Please, Please Me* (1963), and finished with "Get Back" on *Let It Be* (1970). I sang every lyric to him, off-key but with conviction. My son was a mini-me, and even before it was developmentally appropriate, I wanted to share a legacy of entertainment, hobbies, interests, movies, and music.

His mother suffered minor health complications and needed some extra time in bed to rest, so I took the baby around the corner to his first visit with the pediatrician. When she stepped into the room, it was clear that she was uneasy with my then-wife's absence. Before even beginning the examination, the doctor suggested that the baby wasn't eating enough. It was as if the lack of a mother's breast, at that moment, constituted sufficient evidence of malnourishment. I made a mental note of the pediatrician's narrow-mindedness — her commitment to a fictional narrative about the sanctity and necessity of maternal caretaking. The notion of a metaphysical mother–infant bond preemptively discourages the efforts of well-meaning fathers. Plus, it's been used to legitimize gender inequality, to oppress women, and to limit their freedom. bell hooks writes, "It is very telling that in the wake of feminist movement the patriarchal medical establishment which had previously downplayed breast-feeding suddenly began to be not only positive about breast-feeding, but insistent."[16] The pressure on mothers to breast-feed is so obviously out of proportion with the scientific evidence pointing to its benefits over formula (where clean water is available) that it can only be understood as a move to place more child-rearing responsibility on women.[17] But at the time, I was too focused, excited, and anxious about being a new father to let the doctor's bias bother me.

During those first few weeks, I loved being with my newborn son. It was the early days of e-commerce and I ordered a baby wrap online. The large, colorful swath of earth-green organic cotton twill fabric was marketed as an ancient and essential child-rearing tool, a pivotal object in the evolution of human civilization, an iconic artifact of pure attachment parenting.[18] What luck that it had been adapted and manufactured for modern times! It was complicated to don but very comfortable once you got the folds, drapes, and knots just right. I strapped my son to my chest and headed out to buy groceries and diapers at Target. My son was going to enjoy all the benefits of "nurturing touch." And I felt a kinship with my hunter–gatherer ancestors.[19] It was like I was now a part of the primal lineage of human father figures, harvesting essential sustenance for our family.

Soon, there was even more gear. A wealthy relative gifted us an overpriced modular car-seat/stroller. It was called the Frog, or the Salamander, or some other amphibian species. Presumably it was branded that way because it was a hybrid, engineered so it could adapt to multiple environments. Maybe it was also supposed to hint at some reptilian-brain origin story. So much of the marketing aimed at new parents features a paradoxically techno-utopian form of pseudo-Darwinism. We want a fully medicalized and scientifically endorsed version of child development, but we want it to feel primitive and natural. We're even happy to ignore archaic narratives of gender provided they make us feel like we're raising our kids with the wisdom of our ancient ancestors. Anyway, I learned to transform the overengineered stroller contraption into a pram, and I pushed my son on walks around the neighborhood. Of course, people stopped along the sidewalk to admire the "cute" and "adorable" newborn. I quickly noticed the question that came up over and over again: "Where's his mother?" It was almost like a series of billboards beside the highway. THREE MILES UP AHEAD. EXIT HERE. TURN NOW. Were people trying to tell me that my commitment to fatherhood conflicted with the predominant cultural understanding of mature manhood? Was I supposed to conform to the popular perception, or to resist it? Was there any place for me to find the kind of validation that I'd need to stay motivated on my journey to become an involved, feminist dad? Maybe not. Perhaps it was time to pull off the road.

Fifty-three percent of Americans say that, breast-feeding

aside, mothers do a better job than fathers at caring for a new baby. Forty-five percent say that mothers and fathers do it equally well. Only one percent say that fathers do it better. Folks just assume that biological sex determines one's competence at caretaking, making little allowance for variations among individuals. But there's no data or scientific evidence to support these conclusions. They're based on faith and misconceptions. Today's young dads tend be enthusiastic parents, but only thirty-nine percent believe they're doing a "very good job" raising their kids; compare that with fifty-one percent of mothers. In 2016, dads spent triple the number of hours per week involved in childcare as fathers did in 1965. They also accounted for seventeen percent of all stay-at-home parents, up from ten percent three decades earlier, but still they're not satisfied. A 2017 survey found that sixty-three percent of fathers feel like they don't spend enough time with their children. They cite work obligations as the primary obstacle. There's fierce pressure to conform with the societal expectation that men be hardworking and persistent breadwinners. That's the way we're taught to establish our father figure credentials. We should work weekends and overtime, ruthlessly pursuing wealth and status, to demonstrate our commitment to family.[20]

I know this persona well; I've played this part before. When my second son was born, I was thirty years old. I owned and operated a high-volume diner, located in Philadelphia's famous Reading Terminal Market. I worked six days a week — long hours managing staff, ordering food, tracking inventory, and filling in wherever I was needed. Every Saturday and Sunday morning, waking up before dawn, I cracked about ninety dozen eggs to order, making omelets, flipping them over easy, and plating them with a side of thick bacon and hand-cut home fries. I was great at my job, and I made a lot of money, but I was a terrible husband and not a very good person. At work, I hired people who had just returned from prison. They were living in halfway houses. I felt like I was helping them, but if I'm being honest, it was mostly because their labor was cheap, and they always showed up on time — a requirement of parole. I also sometimes spoke inappropriately to the female employees, blindly reproducing the sexism, misogyny, and locker-room gender essentialism I had witnessed during years of working in restaurant kitchens. Worse still, I engaged in regrettable sexual infidelities, perhaps because it made me feel like an alpha male. It was remarkable how many of my own bad behaviors I could pardon and excuse with the phrase, "It's just business."

Eventually, it all caught up with me. In the weeks following my younger son's birth, I found myself in the early days of what would eventually become a long, devastating depressive episode. Looking into my son's eyes forced me to confront difficult questions about what it means to be a good father and a good man. Was my life organized in a way that modeled the kind of maturity I wanted my children to emulate? How could I tell them to live a life that prioritized positive values and beliefs about equality, dignity, and justice if I prioritized profit, power, and pleasure so highly that I could easily overlook unethical choices as long as I was "providing" for my family? The cognitive dissonance broke me. I closed up completely; I stopped talking to most of my loved ones. I cried every day, usually in the mornings, before work, while drinking coffee and staring absentmindedly through the kitchen window. I'd love to describe how it felt, but I was mostly numb.

After a few months, I sold my stake in the restaurant and pursued a graduate degree in depth psychology. At the time, I was too proud to admit that I needed help, that it was my own lack of mental well-being that motivated my studies. Instead, I lived the old cliché that psychologists are the most screwed up, really just trying to fix themselves. I framed my new academic endeavor as a reasonable career change, a pivot. I considered my weekly sessions with a Jungian analyst to be "supplemental research." I believed I was fine, in control, strong, competent, independent. I stoically joked that I was sure to die young because my midlife crisis came so early. Completely obtuse and unaware of my own contradictions, I scoured the internet for self-help books that dealt with fatherhood from the perspective of archetypal psychology, that explored the role of dad as a meaningful identity. I found very few. There was a wealth of personal development literature, which approached masculinity through mythopoetic, spiritual, essentialist, or psychological lenses, but not much that focused specifically on fatherhood. I suspect that's because men generally equate being a father with being an authority figure. They're expected to always know just what to do; they shouldn't need help, but these days, dads do need help.

According to a 2015 Pew report, fifty-seven percent of

fathers identify parenting as something "extremely important to their identity."[21] But the current conception of fatherhood is misaligned with their reality; it fails to provide men with positive aspirational models, meaningful opportunities for reflection, or healthy psychological grounding. Why? Because today, economic, technological, political, and social norms are all changing. We can see it, particularly in the renegotiation of gender categories. The pronoun *they* was Merriam-Webster's word of the year in 2019 — based on a 313 percent surge in online searches. It was *justice* in 2018, and *feminism* the year before that.[22] The vocabulary necessary to have a conversation about power, oppression, and intersectionality has gone mainstream. Critical perspectives that were once confined mostly to academia and activism are now ubiquitous. Regular folks call out fresh examples of institutional bias during each and every news cycle. The victims of intentional and unintentional gender discrimination — along with others who have suffered oppression, violence, exploitation, and trauma due to centuries of systemic inequality — are angry and vociferous. Change is coming; that much is clear, but the outcome of this inevitable transformation remains indeterminate. It's just a hazy sense of revolution lingering on the horizon of the immediately foreseeable future. This is why fathers are floundering. Dads don't know how to imagine themselves without the privileges and entitlements of patriarchy. As a result, some men have become reactionary. They blame women, mothers, and the "identity politics" of elite liberal college professors like me. They fight political battles against women's reproductive rights because they unconsciously mistake non-cisgender-male bodies as a threat. Of course, the only real threat is a lack of meaningful symbolic grounding, a dearth of father-figure imagery that has been adequately updated to align with the current cultural ethos.

Unfortunately, the ordinary progressive reaction is to demonize the men who use anger and blame to compensate for a sense of uncertainty about the future. Liberal folks are quick to point out how ridiculous and hypocritical some tough guys can be. I get it; it's certainly legitimate to dismiss the idea that entitled men might see themselves as victims. To be clear: I'm not defending them. I know that a credible accusation of sexual violence does not constitute a witch hunt.[23] And I have no desire to justify the loudmouths on Twitter who say "cancel culture" makes it a hard time to be a man. Indeed, it is absurd for men to bemoan losing undeserved privileges in the move toward gender parity, but that doesn't mean we can't acknowledge the fact that it always feels disorienting and destabilizing to give up the narratives that add meaning to our lives. It doesn't matter whether those narratives are right or wrong, true or false, just or unjust — they still constitute the structural integrity of an individual's meaning system. It hurts when old stories crumble.

Stories are crumbling all around us. It's hard to overstate the impact. The patterns and categories we've used to define "self" and "other" are being challenged every day — sometimes for good, sometimes for bad. For instance, how can we know who belongs to which identity category in a digital diaspora, where anyone can find their "tribe"? What do cultural allegiance, heredity, and loyalty even mean now that these ideas can be detached from biology and birthplace? Nobody knows for sure. Connected technologies have completely transformed the ways in which we make sense of our relationships, how we communicate with one another, and our definitions of intimacy. A new global paradigm has forced us to live and work in a world that's organized according to a geopolitical model we can barely comprehend. Sure, the familiar boundaries of statehood sometimes prohibit migrant foot traffic — but information, microbes, and financial assets still move swiftly across borders, unimpeded. Similarly, cross-national supply chains have rearranged the rules of the marketplace. High-speed transportation has disrupted how we perceive the limits of time and space. Algorithms and artificial intelligence have changed the way we think about labor, employment, and productivity. Automation has upset the criteria through which we understand meritocracy and self-worth. Data and privacy issues have blurred the boundaries of personal sovereignty. Advances in bioengineering have shaken up the very notion of human nature. It's an existential nightmare. All things considered, it's a safe bet that family and fatherhood will also need to change at the same scale and scope as everything else that constitutes our social and cultural reality.

The problem is that so far, we've resisted all but the most superficial adjustments to family life. Sure, we're happy to add Siri, Alexa, or the Google Assistant into our routines — let her turn the kitchen lights on and off — but we stubbornly resist making any changes to our common understanding of what constitutes a healthy home.[24] We remain fiercely committed to the binary-gendered parenting roles that were established at the beginning of capitalism — back when industrial market economies had just begun to replace artisan craftsmen and family farms. At that time, the cold mechanized efficiency of factory manufacturing and the shiny plate glass of high-rise office buildings introduced an earlier era of disorienting social and cultural transformation. To maintain a sense of psychological stability, people had to somehow make the shift away from an agrarian lifestyle feel "natural." So we adopted a sexist origin story about homemakers and hunters, claiming that the new gender roles were a result of biology and evolution. This is where we get the image of barefoot and pregnant housewives, crouched over kitchen stoves, sweeping and scrubbing. Despite what you may have been told, this particular gendered division of labor — dividing us up into nurturers and breadwinners — is a unique invention of modernity.[25]

In the pre-industrial world, food was too scarce to have half the population staying home to tend the hut. Everyone needed to be a provider — hunting, gathering, farming, whatever it took. Sure, dads often went to war, leaving Mom alone to fulfill *both* roles, but it's not until the nineteenth century that the workplace becomes predominantly male. "A homosocial environment" is what Michael Kimmel, one of the leading academic sociologists specializing in men's studies, calls it. "A male-only world in which he pits himself against other men."[26] Kimmel is referring to the way the masculine workplace became detached, rational, and competitive because the feminine home was seen as altruistic, compassionate, and nurturing. "Self-reliance worked for *men* because *women* took care of dependence and obligation," writes historian Stephanie Coontz. "For both men and women, this meant specialization in one set of behaviors, skills, and feelings at the cost of suppressing others."[27] In other words, the industrial workplace was dependent on the repressive, homophobic aggression that's now called toxic masculinity.

According to a 2019 article in the *New York Times*, toxic masculinity involves suppressing feelings, masking distress, maintaining a macho appearance of hardness, and using violence to hide vulnerability.[28] The diagnosis was formalized in 2018, when the American Psychological Association (APA) issued its first *Guidelines for Psychological Practice with Boys and Men*.[29] That document says that men are so afraid of appearing weak or "feminine" that they bury their feelings; they over-conceal. This can lead to mental health issues, cardiovascular problems, substance abuse, violence, incarceration, early mortality, and more. Surely we'd like to avoid these negative outcomes, but it's foolish to imagine that toxic masculinity is simply an individual's psychological problem. No, this is not something we can solve with cathartic drum circles and nature retreats.[30] To think otherwise just reinforces the same old patriarchal narrative of stoic self-reliance. Instead, we need to understand and deconstruct toxic masculinity within the broader economic, professional, and familial contexts.

We also need to acknowledge that carelessly abandoning the constrictive personas of Industrial Age manhood poses its own kind of risk. What happens to a man's sense of self? He can't discard *all* the tight, delineating signifiers of masculinity at one time. After all, identity is as much about what one holds in as about what one lets out. Boundaries don't just limit and constrain; they also provide definition and form. We can't shed the old symbols without reimagining them in new ways. Otherwise, we'll leave dads in an especially troublesome bind.

Luke, I Am Your Father

It's unfortunate that almost all the common images of fatherhood available to today's men reinforce Industrial Age attitudes about sex and gender. The first one that comes to my mind is the bumbling idiot Homer Simpson. He's a hyperbolic example of the all-too-common clueless and out-of-touch sitcom dad. Sure, he's kind-hearted and well-meaning — ultimately a good man — but he's also silly and incompetent. Plus, he normalizes the violent aggression that stereotypically characterizes the relationship between fathers and sons. Think of the iconic image of Homer strangling Bart. Arms in the air, cartoon tongues wagging, Homer screams, "Why, you little…!"

Who doesn't love Homer? Who can't relate to him? He's an American everyman. As an audience, we tolerate his blatant portrayal of child abuse because we know it's just a cartoon gag. Comedy often depends on dramatizing taboos, revealing inclinations too naughty for real life. Of course, there's nothing wrong with laughing at farce, but when we're done enjoying the Simpsons' antics, we should consider why we accept representations of violent fathering without questioning them. Then we'd see that we've all bought into a tough-love image of paternal responsibility that may have made sense during the Industrial Age but urgently needs to be reinvented for a changing world.

To be a feminist dad, you need to understand that the current image of male psychology remains rooted in old Freudian theory. Freud described a boy's early relationship with his parents using Sophocles's ancient Greek tragic drama *Oedipus Tyrannus* as the model. I'm sure you've heard of the Oedipus complex. Freud developed and expanded the concept over the course of his career, but he first wrote about it in a letter to his friend Wilhelm Fliess, and then in his 1899 book, *The Interpretation of Dreams*.[31] He said that all boys were like the king of Thebes, destined to murder our fathers and marry our mothers. Don't take it literally; understand it symbolically. It's not that the child wants to have incestuous sex with his mother; it's that he desires to maintain an intimate union, characterized by physical dependency. The infant son was once within Mom's body, and now he continues to depend on her breasts for food. Dad is perceived as an obstacle; he stands in the way of the son's ability to satisfy every desire, on demand, through the mother's body. From Freud's perspective, that's because Mother is Father's sexual property; her body belongs to Dad. Son recognizes this and therefore aspires to become like Father. He wants to be a powerful man, able to satiate his own desires and to deny other men the opportunity to satiate theirs. Son wants to accumulate and protect his own sexual property, so he transfers the infantile desire — maternal dependency — onto a new motherlike figure. He finds a wife, and buys a home, and starts a family.

From then on, while Mother maintains a warm, comfortable, nurturing nest, Father goes off to work. There, it's a world of constant competition. Fathers should do everything we can to prove that we're real men: strong and powerful. We show off our ability to possess female sexual objects, as well as goods and status. Think: trophy wives, fast cars, and luxury super boxes in sporting arenas. It's posturing. We constantly flaunt every entitlement because the capitalist industrial economy of the twentieth century — fueled by an advertising industry that was heavily influenced by Freud's nephew, Edward Bernays — taught us to derive our sense of masculine self-worth from wealth and power. We measure our identities in tangible goods and services. It might be a giant tank-like SUV or a pickup truck. It might be an enormous house on a large plot of land in an exclusive community. This version of manhood is as much about the accumulated goods inside that McMansion as it is about demonstrating what we're capable of keeping out. It's also a persona designed to show dominance — to exhibit the power some men have, not only over women and children but also over other men. Why? Because, according to Freud, we're permanently suffering from the original Oedipal trauma of losing access to the maternal breast, and therefore we constantly display our capacity not only to possess objects of desire but also to symbolically castrate the competition, to push other men down, to render them impotent.

To understand how deep this goes, how common this story is, look at *Star Wars*. George Lucas drew his inspiration for the iconic film series from the work of the uber-influential mythologist Joseph Campbell. "I started doing more strenuous research on fairy tales, folklore, and mythology," Lucas explained. "I started reading Joe's books."[32] It wasn't until after Lucas had finished producing all three movies in the original series that he finally met Campbell. The two men quickly became good friends. During the late 1980s, Lucas invited Bill Moyers to film Moyers's interview series with Campbell at the super-private and ultra-exclusive Skywalker Ranch in Marin County, California. *The Power of Myth* was assembled from more than forty hours of interviews with the Obi-Wan Kenobi of comparative mythology himself. You've probably seen clips on YouTube. When the series originally aired on PBS, just after Campbell died, it became "one of the most popular programs in the history of public television."[33] It also brought Campbell's work into the mainstream.

I'm guessing you've heard of the hero's journey. Who hasn't? Derivative versions of Campbell's structuralist monomyth have made their way into just about every niche of the self-help market: writing, weight loss, leadership, spiritual transformation, marketing, branding, and more. Each promises a foolproof algorithm — a kind of supernatural aid, a secret code, a treasure map, a lightsaber — that will maximize engagement, success, fulfillment, and/or profit. Look for the call to adventure. Walk the road of trials. Escape the belly of the whale. Follow your bliss! Unfortunately, few of these hero's-journey offshoots acknowledge that Campbell grafted his multicultural survey of hero myths onto Freud's Oedipus complex. Therefore, the model privileges a problematic narrative of an adolescent psychology that's defined in relationship to a flawed father-figure identity. Now we're all Luke Skywalker, destined to unconsciously direct phallic hostility toward our fathers, but also learning that it's "toxic" when we succumb to the aggressive, dark tendencies of the Force. It's a recipe for anxiety and self-loathing.

Campbell described the battle between hero and tyrant this way: "Whether he knows it or not, and no matter what his position in society, the father is the initiating priest through whom the young being passes on into the larger world." He's talking about cognitive and social-emotional development in a general sense here. The hero's journey is not only about comparing folktales or archetypal patterns. It also metaphorically describes a supposedly healthy path toward psychological maturity, but notice that Campbell presumes the young hero to be male. It's really a boy's journey and it necessarily includes a confrontation with a father figure.[34] Campbell lays out the archetypal rivalries: "the son against the father for the mastery of the universe, and the daughter against the mother to *be* the mastered world."[35] A sexist, patriarchal, binary, misogynistic hierarchy is built right into the monomyth. Fathers and sons battle. According to Campbell, this reflects an inescapable fact about real-life experience: Men are destined to compete for the alpha position in a gendered social hierarchy, which has space for only one dominant male authority.

"We all know a boy can't daddy until his daddy's dead," Maria Dahvana Headley writes in her 2020 translation of the Old English epic *Beowulf*.[36] Clearly, in the mythological realm, the stakes of patrilineage are high. The symbolic struggle between father and son carries both individuals right up to the brink of death, and across the threshold of rebirth. The childish, subordinate, dependent part of every boy must die so that he can be reborn as a dominant patriarch, and the father must surrender his kingdom, a metaphorical death to life as he knows it. "However strong a man may be," the late, great anthropologist Jean-Pierre Vernant wrote about this mythological trope, "however powerful, intelligent, regal, and sovereign, the day comes when time does him in, when age weighs him down, and when, consequently, the offspring he created, the little tyke he used to bounce on his knee and protect and nourish, becomes a man who is stronger than his father and is destined to take his place."[37] In this framework, the abdication of authority functions as both a paternal responsibility and a rite of passage. In other words, the good father should always be training his son for the concluding battle of childhood, but he should also be prepared to accept his destiny. After all, a wise old man is one who has come to terms with becoming a vanquished ruler.

Clearly, this narrative resonates with our modern conception of the father–son relationship. Think: adolescent rebels versus aging seniors. *Okay, Boomer!* It's the generation gap in its most essential manifestation. Therefore, you should also recognize the Industrial Age fetish for innovation, and the

American obsession with political revolution. Likewise, this archetypal story is lurking in our business and professional preoccupation with technological disruption, and it's in the capitalist consumer fixation on novelty: We always want the newest, fastest, flashiest, and most powerful products. We aim to trade our aging goods for youthful replacements because all young heroes must eventually replace elderly fathers and kings — we expect the insurgent to become the establishment, we expect the margin to become the center. Undoubtedly, this is a natural and cyclical inclination that humans sometimes have, but not always. The notion that this story constitutes a universally applicable psychological schema — an essential law of human nature that transcends cultural and historical context — comes directly from Freud. While Dr. Sigmund may be considered outdated, debunked, and scientifically invalid, there's no denying that we still take an astounding number of his theories for granted, especially when it comes to the formative relationships between children and their parents. Consider that there are plenty of primary myths that tell a variety of tales about fathers and sons — Abraham and Isaac, Odysseus and Telemachus, Shiva and Ganesha — but because Freud chose Oedipus, because Campbell followed Freud, and because Lucas followed Campbell, we continue to understand masculine child development through a singular lens of murderous ascendancy.

Of course, Campbell and Lucas aren't uniquely responsible. There are innumerable influences that inadvertently maintain the authority of Freud's flawed theory. Still, when you think about how many of today's boys bond with their fathers while sitting on the sofa watching *Star Wars*, it becomes an especially compelling example of how a narrative of patrilineage manages to maintain its legitimacy as a psychological construct. It demonstrates the subtle way that pop culture can reinforce not only expectations, but also a moral imperative for fathers to enact all the constituent elements of toxic masculinity. Dads are expected to be bad-tempered, guarded, and authoritarian. Rarely emotive. Never vulnerable. After all, they are locked in a battle for survival, armed with blasters and lightsabers. The son is destined to destroy the Death Star (*Star Wars*). So emotional neglect is metaphorically akin to leaving a swaddled baby boy to die in the forest (*Oedipus Tyrannus*). It's not only an act of self-defense but also steadfast stewardship. Dad is just protecting his clan: mother and daughter! He may want to be a caring, committed role model for his sons — what Campbell called "the initiating priest of masculinity" — but even then, acts of paternal abandonment and aggression are still necessary. Tough love supposedly helps sons develop the persistence and tenacity required to succeed in a dog-eat-dog world. Why else do you think Darth Vader cuts off Luke Skywalker's hand? The wound is symbolic of the belief that only pain, conflict, and injury can build character. Boys must be weaned from their mothers; they must learn to reject dependency and embrace fierce individualism. It's the only way for them to become effective father figures themselves.

This Freudian narrative of hero masculinity remains a ubiquitous presence in our popular understanding of developmental psychology — and it's not just the boys. It persists across gender and sexuality. Think of the resistance to so-called helicopter parenting, the worry that coddled college kids aren't learning how to confront triggering ideas, or the belief that we learn only through failure. These examples all illustrate our commitment to the idea that the nurturing ordinarily associated with maternal care is problematic for a growing child. No smothering! Dependence must be disrupted by a reality that's tough, cold, and mythologically masculine. Motherhood equals abundance, fatherhood equals scarcity. Mom loves unconditionally, Dad withholds affection. No wonder the pediatrician thought my newborn son was hungry and malnourished! She assumed, as so many of us do, that even if the good father wants to be custodial — that is, motivated by a desire to defend, protect, mentor, and initiate — he will still provide his children with some amount of hostile, narcissistic, and suppressive antagonism. After all, to develop grit and resilience, a child requires a father figure who mirrors the real world's apathy and indifference.

This is the narrative lingering in everything a dad learns about how to adequately prepare his child for the future. It's built in to our customs from the beginning. Consider the symbolic implications of having Dad snip the umbilical cord in the delivery room. As comedian Michael Ian Black writes in his 2020 book-length letter to his son, "Your mom had held you tight for nine months, and now my first job as your father was to separate you from her? I didn't want to do it, nor did I want to say no because saying no would have, I thought, made the doctor and nurses question my manliness."[38] Freud's Oedipal assumptions have become a routine part of every father's identity as a parent, but they don't necessarily resonate with the way he wants to imagine himself, especially not in the current culture—which seems to be on a trajectory toward a post-patriarchal worldview.

To be a feminist dad, you have to be willing to interrogate these taken-for-granted assumptions; and you have to be ready to reimagine your dad persona in anti-sexist ways.

How It's Always Been

Some people believe that all civilizations are patriarchal, that order itself depends on dominion and obedience, and that hierarchy is inherently paternal. Maybe they point to the New Testament (Matthew 6:9–13), where Jesus lays out The Lord's Prayer (the Paternoster): *Our Father, who art in heaven, hallowed be thy name.* Maybe they point to the Hebrew prayer—*Our Father, Our King; Avinu Malkeinu* (אָבִינוּ מַלְכֵּנוּ)—traditionally recited on Judaic High Holy Days. In the Abrahamic religious traditions, God is father.[39] Some folks equate old texts with history and say, "This is how it's always been. Men are supposed to be in charge."

In all fairness, despite what some feminist writers would have you believe, there's not conclusive evidence that pure, matriarchal societies have ever existed, but that doesn't really prove anything. Why not? Because there's not conclusive evidence that pure, patriarchal societies existed, either. Each culture, throughout time, has had its own unique ways of thinking about gender. History's patriarchal societies didn't look exactly like ours. To suggest otherwise would be to take great extrapolative liberty. Culture is always changing. You know this is true because even during the relatively short history of the United States, we've renegotiated our gender categories multiple times. Today, men's and women's roles in secular society bear little resemblance to what my great-grandfather would've expected. The point is it's not an either/or situation. There's no eternal battle being waged between patriarchy and matriarchy. There's no competition between men and women to claim all the power and authority. Therefore, we don't need evidence of polarized opposites because we know that reality exists on a spectrum. Besides, even at times when systemic misogyny organizes human civilization, women are still an integral part of what it means to be a man. "Being a man first and foremost," writes Brown University anthropology professor Matthew Gutmann, "means not being a woman."[40] In other words, gender has been defined through contrasts and comparisons that lead to restrictions and permissions. We establish spiritual, professional, and parental duties according to unsubstantiated proclamations about intrinsic difference, and then we point to fictional origin stories, declaring old myths to be evidence of natural law. It's logistics and bureaucracy based on faith. It never holds up under serious scientific or philosophical scrutiny, which is why societies are always changing.

To drive this point home, let's take a look at the science. First, understand the difference between gender and sex. Gender is the word that's often used to describe the traits, characteristics, and experiences that are associated with identity. Sex is the word used to describe one's biological anatomy. This serves a useful distinction for scholars, theorists, and writers who work on feminist and LGBTQ+ issues.[41] However, it's imperfect and somewhat problematic — but not for the reasons you may think. It's not the notion of fluid and nonbinary gender identities that's flawed. No, by design, theoretical categories maintain their integrity even when confronted with the subjective uncertainty and philosophical ambiguity of reality. Instead, it's the deterministic ways we try to box tangible, natural phenomena into simple classifications; that's what ultimately crumbles under rigorous examination. In other words, science reveals that there is no clear, comprehensive binary when it comes to biological sex.

Surely, some readers will protest. After all, we're taught from a very young age that boys have penises and girls have vaginas. You can see the difference, right? Not always. Researchers estimate that one or two out of every hundred people are born intersex, meaning they're born with sexual or reproductive anatomy that cannot be characterized using simple binary criteria.[42] If you're not a statistician, you may think that one or two percent makes these people outliers, abnormalities, or oddities. It doesn't. One or two percent is a lot! That's about the same number of people who are born with green eyes or red hair — significantly more than the percentage of fathers who are likely to buy a Budweiser after viewing a single Super Bowl commercial. Do we think of certain hair or eye colors as "medical conditions" or "aberrations"? No. We acknowledge that, although these characteristics don't apply to ninety-eight percent of people, they still represent natural, expected variations in the basic human experience.

Of course, folks who are resistant to the idea of a fluid spectrum will probably accuse me of cherry-picking numbers from studies that support my argument. After all, it is true that the percentage rate of intersex births is often contested. Some researchers think the real number is much lower than one to two percent.[43] They point out that if you look at ambiguous genitalia alone, it's only about half of one percent. Chromosomal, hormonal, and other variations make up the difference, but it seems to me that if the criteria used to classify intersex can be so easily disputed — if experts argue about how to define the category that doesn't fit our categories — then their disagreement is itself just another indication that a straight binary isn't working.

To make this clearer, let's consider chromosomal variation.[44] If you took biology in high school, you probably learned that XX equals female and XY equals male. Did you know that there is only a single gene (SRY) on the Y chromosome that determines reproductive anatomy? SRY is a protein that binds to specific regions of DNA, causing a fetus to develop testes, and preventing it from developing a uterus and fallopian tubes. So, having the SRY gene means you're genetically "male" and presumably capable of being a dad, but in some mutations — and there are many — SRY doesn't behave as expected.[45] The fetus develops female reproductive organs despite having typically male chromosomes. Likewise, it's possible for the SRY gene to jump onto the X chromosome, leading to the opposite effect: testes without a Y chromosome.[46] Think about what that means: It's possible to be born with the chromosomes culturally associated with being female, and the reproductive anatomy that's necessary to biologically father a child.

Next, consider hormones. Everybody knows about testosterone. We're told that it's what causes boys to be aggressive, horny, entrepreneurial, and assertive. It's why fathers are in charge, right? Supposedly, testosterone is the endocrine essence of masculinity, the male counterpart to the female estrogen. These hormones are not actually sex- or gender-specific. Estrogen plays a critical role in the male body — even in the penis. It's involved in erectile function, libido, and the production of sperm.[47] Likewise, testosterone is key to the healthy functioning of a female body; it's produced in the ovaries, adrenal glands, fat cells, and skin cells. And while it's true that bodies typically considered to be female, on average, produce much less testosterone than bodies typically considered to be male, that small amount can have huge effects.[48] Also, some women have exceptionally high levels of testosterone and some men have exceptionally low levels. Consider one recent study that showed that "one in six elite male athletes have testosterone levels below the normal reference range."[49] In some cases, the levels among these uber-macho sports heroes were even lower than the average among elite female athletes. This is just one among many studies that have conclusively demonstrated that the characteristics culturally associated with masculinity and femininity don't track to a simple hormonal dyad. Our sex and gender categories are really just fantasies — imperfect linguistic tools that we use to organize a chaotic universe in ways that feel familiar and palatable. The truth is much more complicated, and that becomes clear when you recognize that it's possible to be chromosomally male or female, and hormonally nonbinary.

Do you have any idea what your own testosterone level is? How about the way your chromosomes are mapped? I don't know anything about either, and yet I choose to identify as a man. I use the pronouns he/him. That's my prerogative. I didn't need a test to prove it was true. If I took one, I'd likely discover things I didn't know. Yet my privileged position in society entitles me to call myself whatever I want. Doesn't everyone deserve the freedom to make that choice? I think so. I also choose to identify as a father. The question in this book is: What does that really mean? Certainly, it's true that I produced the sperm that fertilized the eggs that ultimately became the embryos of my children.[50] Now they call me Dad, but what does that have to do with the way I relate to them, the way I imagine myself, the part I choose to act out on a daily basis? Is my early-morning anger and aggression related to hormone levels? Is it chromosomes that lead me to check "head of household" on my federal income taxes? No. Scientists can't even prove that biological sex determines gender identity, let alone parental inclinations.

And yet so many of us continue to believe that the role of a father is fixed and innate. Not me. I'm not interested in gender essentialism, not the biological version or the psychological one. I even reject the idea that archetypal images of masculinity can transcend their cultural and historic contexts. Despite my background in Jungian depth psychology, I don't believe that the old mythopoetic perspective — originally popularized by Robert Bly's *Iron John* Men's Movement of the 1980s and '90s — is an adequate solution to the crisis of identity that today's dads face. Those who identify as men should not anchor themselves in outdated, formulaic personae. It makes no sense to try to act like warriors, wizards, and Casanovas.[51] Boys don't need to toughen up, stand up straight,[52] and find their inner athletes, alchemists, and pickup artists. Dads don't need to be tyrants, judges, executioners, and holy men.

To be a feminist dad, you need to acknowledge that it's time to reinvent the father figure for a new era. Before we can do so, we need to recognize the way popular stories, images, and attitudes have made arbitrary conventions seem like natural facts of life. Roland Barthes once called this "the decorative display of what-goes-without-saying."[53] A popular French essayist who wrote about literature and pop culture at the end of the twentieth century, he resented the way taken-for-granted structures end up shaping our aspirations. He tried to expose the way certain elements of our everyday experience orient our assumptions about who we can be and how we can imagine ourselves. Barthes called this "ideological abuse."[54] He argued that whenever we blindly accept things as ordinary, normal, or natural, we're simultaneously fortifying a subjective social structure, and therefore limiting our potential to create other possibilities. In other words, he thought cultural narratives promoted certain meanings by hiding the alternatives.

In the rest of this book, I will identify some of the taken-for-granted narratives and images that contour our expectations, and I'll unveil some of the alternatives. I hope to offer an aspirational image of a new kind of father figure—one that's less paternal, less dominant, less narcissistic, and not necessarily masculine. It's an image that's better attuned to the current cultural moment. It illustrates that there's a different kind of caretaking role that fathers can play in the lives of their children. There's also a different kind of parental identity that dads can integrate into their experience of becoming mature adults. I've chosen to use he/him pronouns when referring to "father" because that's how I think of myself, but I don't mean to exclude anyone who identifies differently.

The new father figure begins his journey by acknowledging that he is not necessarily the family's chief executive officer—that life need not be experienced as a narcissistic bedtime story in which the patriarch is always the protagonist. Dad is not a king waiting to be dethroned by the young hero in an epic competition for dominance. He's not a wealthy proprietor who's principally concerned with how lines of patrilineage influence the perpetuity of his estate. He is not the guardian of his daughter's virginity; her body and her psychosexual development are not a realm in which he needs to exercise authority. Finally, he doesn't need to see himself as a disciplinarian or a repairman because everything doesn't need to be fixed and solved. Instead, paternal leadership can be responsive and participatory. Dad can acknowledge that we are all just the unreliable narrators of our own personal fairy tales.[55] No single story is more important than the others. A father may indeed be the protagonist of his own myth, but he knows that he's also someone's villain, and someone else's mentor. Therefore, he shouldn't be surprised, hurt, or resistant when he discovers he's been cast in roles that he didn't sign up for. His primary duty is to play those parts well.

PART TWO

OUR FATHER, OUR KING

SUNDAY, 2:45 P.M.: Big, heavy water droplets slam against the windows. Real thunderstorms sound much more authentic than the white noise I usually stream from the internet.

I once had a student whose midterm PowerPoint presentation described himself as a "pluviophile," a person who loves the rain. I don't think it's a real word. After class, thumbs pecking at my smartphone as I walked across campus, I looked it up online. There were a bunch of semi-satirical blog-listicles and a few You-Tube videos that used the term, but I couldn't find anything in the Oxford English Dictionary that linked *pluvial* (relating to rain) with *philia* (love, affection, or fondness). Still, I like it—both the word and the sentiment. A thunderclap of lightning never rattled me. Even as a kid, I found rain quiet, calm, and blissful.

Now that I'm middle-aged, there's no better ambience for curling up on the sofa and reading a novel.

Today I'm gripping a new book by an old friend from college.[1] I haven't spoken to her in a few years, but we regularly admire each other's social media posts. She once created a series of travel selfies in which a plush toy elephant named Titus accompanied her on a tour of Italy — riding gondolas, eating risotto, strolling through the Villa Borghese. Her status updates make me laugh. I click the thumbs-up, the heart, the smiley face. She seems to do the same for me. Unfortunately, I'm struggling to make my way through each paragraph of her novel. It feels like I've read the same sentence nineteen times — the same phrases, the same words, the same jokes. It's not her fault. The prose is incisive; she's a talented author. I read everything she publishes. The problem is my younger son. He won't stop bothering me.

"Dad, can I ask you a question?" He bursts into the room every few minutes. "Can I tell you what happened in my video game?" He's grabbing my arm, tugging and pulling. "Do you know why the Wi-Fi is *so* laggy?!"

At first, I try to reason with him, "C'mon, dude, can you give me like thirty minutes to myself? I'm tryin' to read something."

He wanders down the hallway, fingertips dirtying the paint on the wall as he turns the corner and disappears into his bedroom. I adjust the throw pillow behind my head, pull up the lambswool blanket so it covers my bare legs and read about half a page more before he's looking down at me all over again.

"Dad, what are we having for dinner?"

I lose my temper. *"Are you kidding me with this?!?"*

I raise my voice: a long and loud diatribe about how much time and energy I give to him and his brother. I'm a martyr, dammit. Don't I deserve an occasional lazy rainy afternoon without interruption? What have *you* done for this household today? Why don't you go clean your room? Scrub the toilets? Fold the laundry? Cook dinner? When I was your age, my father made me do *hard* chores!

My son rolls his eyes and mumbles as he walks away. Just one word: Bully.

Lately he's been complaining that I scream too much, but that just makes me yell louder. It bruises my ego and threatens my authority. I'm supposed to be the one who knows best practices, especially when it comes to parenting. I want to be the arbiter of the moral high ground. I don't like when a tween-ager calls out my selfish shortcomings. In these moments — my cheeks hot-red, sweat beading on the back of my neck, hands quivering slightly — I think of Zeus from Greek mythology. He's often portrayed as an authoritarian. He bullies his wife, Hera, and their children.[2] In one story, his son Hephaistos tries to intervene in a marital squabble and Zeus goes nuts. He grabs the boy by the ankle and tosses him off Mount Olympus. Hephaistos falls for a whole day, eventually landing on the island of Lemnos.

My son recovers from my irrational temper tantrums like Hephaistos recovers from his fall. Of course, Hephaistos is immortal, but he's not impervious to permanent wounds. His body is now disfigured. He walks with a limp, hobbling for all eternity. The story can be understood as a metaphor for the way a human father figure's minor authoritarian actions can cause long-lasting emotional damage. It tells us that the tough-love lessons we try to teach our kids don't stick; they wound. That's why Hephaistos eventually takes up shop in the bowels of a volcano, forging the very thunderbolts that Zeus infamously casts in anger. It's symbolic. The son may seem content, but he lives a tragic fate. He fashions objects of unparalleled craftsmanship: the armor and provisions of gods and heroes. The artistry is so elaborate that it takes Homer 150 lines of *Iliad* to describe the shield of Achilles: "heavy and huge, every inch of it intricately designed...glittering like lighting."[3] Similar to many modern workaholics, Hephaistos is always trying to prove his worth; his labor and dedication are perversely linked to the trauma he suffered at the hands of a rageful father.

Now I'm imagining my son, full-grown, limping silently around an office building or a factory, trying to earn my approval. It breaks my heart. I put down my book and give him my undivided attention. Some folks may think it's the wrong decision. They see the story of Hephaistos, along with other examples of Zeus's tyrannical disposition, as validation for the authority that human fathers often have over their families. They argue that Zeus's exploits are evidence that absolute patriarchal power is an essential, archetypal force that's been associated with fatherhood and masculinity since time immemorial. They see Greek mythology as proof that Dad is supposed to be an uncompromising disciplinarian, but these viewpoints are wrong. For one thing, mythological precedent is a bad justification for modern behavior. More to the point, this perspective represents a biased understanding of Zeus's bullying thunderbolts. Watch out for interpretations like these, which superimpose the logic of Eurocentric monotheism onto Hellenic polytheism. You can't just appropriate the ancient artifacts of one religious system to validate the patriarchal inclinations of another.

Zeus and his thunderbolts are not evidence that "masculine" patriarchal dominance is a legitimate and natural part of the human experience. The Greek pantheon does not exemplify that kind of singular monarchy. "Zeus posits himself above all others, for the archetypal idea of oneness presents itself as first, superior, progenitor," wrote the American archetypal psychologist James Hillman, "But Zeus is just one among other equals."[4] Each of the Olympian immortals has their own special sovereignty. Each has their own goal, their own energetic tone, their own realm of power. Zeus is the deity who sometimes displays an inclination toward tyrannical force. He sees himself as the autocratic ruler of the gods, but the ancient humans who wrote the stories didn't see him that way.

In their texts, there's no competition to climb the ladder of the Olympian corporate structure; no other gods challenge Zeus's rule, yet nothing terrifies him more than murderous ascendancy. That's why he's always defending his status. In this way, he reminds me of the stereotypical entry-level Wall Street banker — sporting a too-shiny tailored suit and a bright grenadine silk tie, boasting about alpha-male achievements that the rest of us find unimpressive. Similarly, the other Olympians are uninterested in Zeus's dominion. They're too focused on alternative kinds of power. They know that executive will does not always reign supreme. In fact, there are many myths in which Zeus's narcissistic love of autocratic force becomes his fatal flaw. He's sometimes outwitted by Athena or seduced by Aphrodite. That's because Zeus is not a model from which humans should deduce the criteria for good behavior. The ancient Greeks didn't have bumper stickers that said WHAT WOULD ZEUS DO? No, he's a cautionary figure, a symbol that warns us how dangerous it can be to rely exclusively on the power that comes from hurling thunderbolts.

It's not that thunderbolts don't have their place. After all, to a pluviophile, they're blissful and calm. The popular Vietnamese Thiền Buddhist monk Thich Nhat Hanh evokes them while teaching about the power of quiet, compassionate listening: "There are times when silence is truth, and that is called 'thundering silence.' "[5] Clearly, there are both positive and negative qualities associated with thunderbolts. To be a feminist dad, you need to identify the good stuff and be wary of the bad.

From a mythopoetic perspective, thunderbolts can represent our capacity to make singular and pointed decisions. Zeus's thunderbolts can be a metaphor for strong, clear, and determined action. He is a leader, an executive who can target problems and solve them quickly. Please don't jump to the conclusion that these positive traits are innate characteristics of fatherhood or masculinity. The ancient Greeks saw Zeus-like attributes as a universal choice — sometimes necessary and unavoidable — but not an innate predisposition unique to certain categories of people. Sure, Zeus favored some heroes, but more often than not his favor brought tragedy.

Remember, the ancient Greeks had many gods, and too much attention given to or received from any one of the immortals was considered problematic. It was like a curse. In modern times, archetypal psychologists frame this problem as the "ego fallacy."[6] It's what happens when we overidentify with a single mythological figure. Understand that in classical Jungian thought, each character in a myth represents a specific cognitive outlook or emotional temperament. The stories describe how different psychological energies, or complexes, interact with one another. Like the colorful sprites in Disney Pixar's 2015 animated feature *Inside Out*, the characters in myth are personifications of internal drives, moods, complexes, and mental dispositions. Therefore, one of the messages you can infer from interpreting most ancient Greek myths in this way is that too much or too little from any single voice is problematic.

Psychological well-being requires that inner forces cooperate, that they make decisions by consensus, that they're equally represented. The ego fallacy is what happens when one inner voice becomes dominant — when it defines an individual's identity. "Not only does this identification 'egoize' one of the figures in a myth," writes NYU professor and Jungian analyst Michael Vannoy Adams, "it also tends to normalize that figure and pathologize the other figures."[7] What he means is that it makes us believe one set of attitudes and behaviors is right and proper, while all possible deviations from it are wrong and improper. Consider this lesson in the context of father figures. It tells us that an important part of becoming a feminist dad is learning to avoid an ego fallacy. Be cautious not to overidentify with certain expressions of the familiar dad persona. Don't aspire to a singular, comprehensive, absolute, and immutable image of the father figure. That's the very definition of ego-fallacy autocracy.

"Masculine" patriarchal authority — garrisoned with domination, violence, and thunderbolts — is not something universal and innate, and all potential alternatives to it are not pathological. That is the fallacy folks are trying to uphold each time they say, "A child needs a strong masculine influence in their lives." They want us to believe that healthy development depends on toxic paternal force, that anything unorthodox will hurt our children. A feminist dad knows that this is not true. You can, and should, make different choices. Recognize that you can be a leader, a boss, and even a disciplinarian some of the time; but you shouldn't be any of those things all the time. Evaluate the specific situations in which you find yourself, analyze the context, and call on the deity, disposition, or inner voice most appropriate for the job at hand. In other words, be responsive.

Make It So

To be a feminist dad, you need to abandon the singular notion of "masculine," patriarchal authority and replace it with the multifaceted and polyvalent concept of non-gendered, humanistic responsibility. To understand what this entails, consider the basic differences between authority and responsibility.

Authority is about power. Responsibility is about duty. Authority is often forceful and coercive. Responsibility, as superstar self-help guru Stephen Covey suggests, is just what it sounds like: being able to respond.[8] A father shouldn't have authority over his family; he must have response-ability for them.

All the research shows that an empathetic, child-centered approach to parenting is more effective than a rigid, disciplinary one. Everything you've heard about fixed versus growth mindset, intrinsic versus extrinsic motivation, and positive versus negative reinforcement points in this direction. Carrots work better than sticks. Spanking causes more harm than good. Shame leads to long-lasting psychological trauma. Punishments like time out and grounding are effective only as interventions, not as a way to encourage long-term behavioral change. The old fear-based parenting methods don't work. You and I turned out all right despite — not because of — constant scolding and an occasional smack. Not everyone was so lucky. It's time for dads to stop letting physical force and emotional coercion be their default choice and adopt a more responsive approach. The biggest challenge will be abandoning the paternalistic, father-knows-best style of offering guidance. Dads must recognize that we sometimes deliver advice in a manner that belittles children's agency and sends the wrong message about competence and expertise. Witness, listen, and support your child's unique journey instead. Being responsible means modeling creative problem-solving skills, intellectual humility, a fluid conception of maturity, and a commitment to lifelong learning.

But becoming a feminist dad is about more than just the techniques adults should use to motivate their children. It's also about shifting your mindset, and approaching fatherhood identity from an anti-sexist perspective. How can men be better father figures by moving away from the habitual thought patterns of patriarchy? The answer lies beyond the popular discourse on being a good man. Sure, it's true that less dad-bullying means less toxic masculinity, but the transition from authority to responsibility involves much more than just familiar buzzwords and hashtag-worthy diagnostics. It also requires acknowledging that a taken-for-granted commitment to coercive force subtly pervades the bulk of our thinking. We need to let go of it, but doing so is challenging because, as I'll explain in the coming pages, we admire the patriarchal mindset so profoundly that it ends up misinforming many of the viewpoints that we ordinarily consider to be kind, compassionate, and transformative. Therefore, even when we try to do the right thing, we often misstep.

As we go about our daily lives, a deep reverence for authoritative characteristics and personality traits shapes our basic conception of the individual self. It permeates our popular psychology, self-help, and productivity literature, and it pretty much defines the way we think about agency, autonomy, and personal development. That's a huge problem because it means dads are getting mixed messages. Today's fathers are told constantly — even in this book — that they have a moral and ethical obligation to abandon the sexist stoicism of the 1950s sitcom dad. Say goodbye to the Oedipal symbolism of murderous ascendancy; reject the image of mature manhood as necessarily restrained and impenetrable; and halt the steady unconscious (and sometimes conscious) deployment of homophobia and misogyny. That's all good! The problem is that dads are simultaneously bombarded with another kind of subtle, coded rhetoric. It's on television and the internet, in school and at work, in magazines and on billboards. Pop culture constantly celebrates the idea that everyone, regardless of gender, needs to embody the patterns of old-school paternal authority. Hurl thunderbolts! It's how you succeed.

Just think about the way we praise the tyrannical behavior of popular business leaders. Take Apple founder Steve Jobs, for example. We call him a visionary, glorifying his dictatorial persistence, unwavering commitment, and fierce resistance to contrary opinions. This aspirational nod to predatory domination is not unique to the corporate world. It's paralleled by our admiration for tough, badly behaved athletes. Think of superstar NFL linebacker Dick Butkus ("Every time he hit you, he tried to put you in the cemetery, not the hospital"[9]), tennis legend John McEnroe (he was continually fined and suspended for the angry, foul language he used while contesting the umpire's calls), or iconic NHL center Bobby Clarke (his infamous slash to Soviet player Valeri Kharlamov's ankle during the 1972 Summit Series speaks for itself). You see the same characteristics exhibited by many celebrities, musicians, politicians, and entrepreneurs. Often, folks try to justify their behaviors with the phrase *survival of the fittest*. They want to argue that the tendency toward domination is a biological inevitability, but as author Emily Willingham explains, "Evolutionary psychology, when taken with the false doctrine that evolution is about 'winning,' offers a perfect cover for these aspirants and a perfect tool to perpetuate themselves as 'winners.' "[10] It's just dogma and rhetoric. The truth is that successful reproduction — i.e., the transmission of DNA in accordance with Darwinian theory — works a lot like parenting; the best outcomes have much more to do with adaptability than they do with authority or strength.

Clearly, our ongoing veneration for no-holds-barred, ends-justify-the-means victory contradicts the anti-patriarchal messaging that should now establish the criteria for being a good dad. This ambiguity sets up well-meaning fathers for frustration and failure. Any attempts they make to change the deeply ingrained postures of patriarchal consciousness become riddled with confusion. Why? Because even those who are able to avoid the behaviors and attitudes typically associated with toxic masculinity remain wedded to a definition of autonomy and agency that's intrinsically violent and domineering. Worse still, because most folks barely acknowledge these inherent incongruities, dads lack the vocabulary necessary to proactively resolve the tension, so let's consider this father figure's dilemma in more detail.

Critics, journalists, academics, and authors call out problematic patriarchal messaging with increasing regularity, but the elusive reverence for certain psychological characteristics of paternal force continues to go mostly unnoticed. To see it, start by looking at the definition of *authority*. The word literally means that one is entitled to be an author. I know that's not how we usually use it. Most of the time, we think of authority in terms of power and obedience. We think of it as a kind of force — the act of giving orders or demanding compliance. Maybe you imagine a military general, an angry coach, or a strict teacher. Even these examples are connected to authorship, and not only in the sense that we consider a writer to be "an authority" on their subject matter. Just look at the history of the word *authority*. The familiar, hierarchical connotation comes from twelfth-century Europe, around the same time that humans invented the windmill (more about that later). Back then, authority referred to the idea that certain books or passages of text — usually scripture — were authoritative. That is, they were supposedly written by God himself. He was the author, and therefore the words on the page dictated true and incontestable details about everything under the sun.[11]

People's lives were assembled in response to the images and scenarios contained in divine chapters, verses, sentences, and stanzas. Sure, interpretation was often required — what's technically called biblical exegesis — but after that, everyone was expected to comply fully with heavenly words. Most of the time, folks did so willingly, but have you ever thought about why? It's certainly not because medieval peasants were any more obedient than the average person is today; they weren't stupider, more gullible, or less rebellious. Instead, it's because pre-enlightenment folks thought that contradicting biblical authority was like breaking a law of nature. For them, religious doctrine wasn't a suggestion. They didn't perceive it the way the majority of us do in the secular world: as a recommendation for how one might choose to live a moral life. Instead, people followed the rules because authoritative religious texts claimed to describe fundamental facts about the universe.

When it came to biblical authority in the twelfth century, not conforming with the words on the page constituted an existential aberrance, a crime against the nature of being. To a true believer living in the 1100s, a deviation from the scripture authored by God was tantamount to how you or I — or pretty much any other individual living in current times — would feel if we found a boulder that wasn't subject to the force of gravity. Imagine you're hiking on a trail and you come across a big hunk of deep-blue lapis lazuli. It's mysteriously suspended in the air, four or five feet above the ground. Eerie. Puzzling. Uncanny. I'm guessing you wouldn't call it evil or satanic, but you'd certainly find its existence disorienting and destabilizing. I suspect that before you abandoned everything you learned in your high school physics class, you'd first try to construct a rationalization as to why this one object didn't play by the normal, familiar rules.[12] Maybe there's a magnetic force. Maybe it's just an optical illusion. It's probably not an alien spaceship from another galaxy. Nor is it a prophetic orb sent as a message from Zeus on Olympus. You'd remain committed to the fundamental facts of your scientific worldview, even when confronted with something that blatantly contradicts it.

Remember this big blue boulder, the truths you'd readily accept, and your unwillingness to entertain an alternative viewpoint whenever you read the word *authorize*. It didn't always mean to give permission; it once meant attesting or vouching for the truth of the universe. The power to authorize something was the same as the power to dictate reality itself. It rested in the hands of monarchs, rulers, and clergy — the patriarchs. To us, living in an era where reality is usually established empirically, it may sound crazy and outdated that once upon a time someone could just announce the truth and everyone else would accept it, but there are ways in which authority continues to function in exactly this sense, and not only in the mouths of would-be political autocrats. It's even in our most progressive, futuristic fantasies. Think of Patrick Stewart as Captain Jean-Luc Picard in *Star Trek: The Next Generation*. As he gives an authoritative order to engage the starship *Enterprise*'s warp drive, he points his finger and says his famous catchphrase, "Make it so!" He is not only authorizing the use of a powerful technology but also declaring his right to dictate reality, to make something *be*.

Picard is a father figure. The whole ship's company looks up to him. The *Enterprise* crew is like a big family and Jean-Luc sits at the head of the proverbial dinner table. His scripted catchphrase reinforces this paternal reality, but did you know that the expression he uses is not unique to *Star Trek*? "Make it so" was a command regularly uttered by British naval officers for centuries. I suspect it's inspired by Genesis. God speaks, commanding water to separate from sky, ocean from land, night from day, and each time the same refrain: "And it was so."[13] The holy father made it so, and his actions came to exemplify traditional patriarchal authority.

Consider that the phrase "Make it so" succinctly articulates the underlying assumptions that define coercive power: a superior progenitor has a right to authorize reality — to declare truth, assess value, establish meaning, and compel others to conform to his judgments. In addition, "Make it so" points toward a phenomenon that's not only at the core of how we imagine father figures, but also our predominant understanding of what it means for anyone (of any gender) to consider themselves a mature, autonomous individual. The word *autonomy* comes from the same root as *authority* (αὐτός/*autos* means "self"). It describes personal liberty or individual agency, but usually we use the term in reference to psychological independence, borrowing an idea first articulated by the philosopher Immanuel Kant (1724–1804). Are your actions and choices self-determined, or are they affected by outside forces such as peer pressure, advertising, religious doctrine, government regulation, or parental expectations? For Kant, you weren't autonomous unless you were unencumbered by external influence. Our contemporary understanding of autonomy is still based on Kant's ideas.[14] Consider that most of us believe we have a true self. We all envision some variation on a pure, inner voice that can and should ascertain the truth. Put another way: We believe each individual should have the freedom to frame a subjective view of reality that's in alignment with who they are at the core of their being. You know the social media memes:

We are constantly invited to be who we are! You can't change what's going on around you until you change what's going on within you. Don't be "most people."

From this perspective, to be healthy is to be capable of identifying your own true, unique desire, and to be fulfilled is to be empowered to make it so. The problem — if you want to be a feminist dad — is that this view of autonomy is grounded in *narcissistic patriarchal authority*.

Narcissistic Patriarchal Authority

Once upon a time, an aging father had three sons. Dad is sick, maybe he's dying. Perhaps he's had a prophetic dream. He summons his children.

How many well-known folktales begin this way? At least fifty or sixty just in the Brothers Grimm collection.[15] There is something about the three sons motif that made it especially popular among the storytellers of earlier generations. It has to do with how they thought about Dad's authority. As you'll see, their view has influenced the way we now think about psychological autonomy. Understand that the father is always at the center of these fairy tales. It might seem like these are stories about three children, because Dad spends the whole narrative on his deathbed, but really he is the author of the entire adventure. It's just like how Joseph Campbell's monomyth appears to be about the hero, but it's actually about the way a son takes his rightful place as a father figure. Both the hero's journey and the three-sons motif are about property, legacy, power, and

identity, and therefore they are stories about narcissistic patriarchal authority.

I define *narcissistic patriarchal authority* as the taken-for-
granted assumption that fathers are entitled to determine the
narrative reality impacting everyone around them. Dad's life is
primary, he authors the story, he frames the truth. Therefore,
his subjective interpretations shape everyone else's psychological and somatic experiences. Of course, Dad's narcissistic patriarchal authority is not always explicit. Everyone else may feel
like they're making autonomous choices. Dad may even go out
of his way to encourage members of his family to be independent and empowered. Nevertheless, the implicit bias tilts toward
Dad. He doesn't respond to circumstances; he dictates them.
Like the Old Testament God, he decides what's inscribed in
his family's book of life. He authorizes everything, and his
right to do so is not only at the core of his identity, but also
embedded into our cultural assumptions about the "proper"
organization of a household.

As Friedrich Engels once argued, patriarchal authority and
property ownership was what motivated the development of
monogamous coupling and the independent child-rearing conventions that have gone along with this model of household
organization from the beginning. Engels pointed out that the
original meaning of the word *family* had very little to do with
affection, commitment, or sentimentality. "*Famulus* means
domestic slave, and *familia* is the total number of slaves belonging to one man."[16] That's a far cry from the kind of loyal kinship and unconditional love that our contemporary family

sitcoms tend to celebrate, but it is perfectly aligned with the bedtime stories we tell our children.

The Grimm Brothers' story "The Three Feathers" begins this way: "When the king had become old and weak, and was thinking of his end, he did not know which of his sons should inherit the kingdom."[17] Should it be the oldest? The wise one? He's smart because he reads the right books. He's rational. He gets the nuances of governance, law, and order. He's not easily seduced by idealistic fantasies, but the king knows that his oldest son's prudence might also be a liability. The wise one is exceedingly risk averse—afraid of change, conservative, inflexible. Perhaps this is not the best quality in a monarch. Maybe the middle son is a better choice. He's clever. He's good with money, a great investor, an opportunist. He knows how to hedge his bets. The kingdom will surely expand its wealth and territory under his rule. Yet Dad is hesitant because he recognizes that the clever son can sometimes be hot-headed, too convinced of his own merit, not compassionate enough toward the peasants. As if that weren't complicated enough, the king also wants to consider his youngest, for whom he's always had a special affinity. His youngest is different, an outsider, a black sheep, an ugly duckling—stubbornly unique. He is so committed to nonconformity that he barely even talks to other people. Depending on how you look at it, that can either mean he's creative and reclusive, or stupid and socially inept. Therefore, on his worst days, Dad dismisses his third son as a lazy simpleton. The Swiss psychologist Marie-Louise von Franz called this archetypal character "the Dummling."[18]

Von Franz was one of the most famous Jungian analysts of all time; she worked closely with Carl Jung himself. She's famous for her books and lectures on the psychological symbolism of fairy tales. She didn't see them as trivialities of the nursery. Instead, she approached them as if they were the collective dreams of medieval Europe. She wrote, "Fairy tales are the purest and simplest expression of collective unconscious psychic processes." She argued that because folktales emerge over time — casually told to children at home — they're a kind of spontaneous and uninhibited psychological artifact. "They represent the archetypes in their simplest, barest, and most concise form."[19] Her perspective makes sense when you understand that Jacob and Wilhelm Grimm weren't the authors of their famous fairy tales. No, they wandered the countryside, collecting and recording them. These are the people's stories, oral tales that had been adapted for generations. In each iteration, only certain images and narrative elements would be preserved — only what supported the desires, anxieties, wishes, and worries of the families and communities who continued to tell the tales. That's why these stories should interest us. They can tell us something about how our own unconscious habits of mind came to be — specifically our inclinations toward narcissistic patriarchal authority.

Consider "The Three Feathers" from a Jungian perspective. The setting of a story always symbolizes a psychological way of being. The state of the kingdom equals a state of mind, and since monarchs are the living embodiment of the kingdom — the personification of the political state — an aging, dying king represents an unhealthy and unstable mindset. Therefore, folktales like these seem to be concerned with what happens when one's primary cognitive attitude becomes symptomatic and degenerative. How do we conduct ourselves when old ways of thinking deteriorate? What do we do when the old psychological frameworks no longer provide an adequate structure for meaningful existence? When they're dying? When their authority wanes? When they need to be replaced? It's almost as if these stories were developed to describe the precise situation in which today's fathers find themselves, but as you'll soon see, the solution we've come to consider normal and healthy is inadequate for the current cultural moment.

Here's what happens: The king knows it's time for a change and he looks at the menu of options before him. He sees his three sons. Each represents a different youthful mentality, a particular outlook on the world, a cognitive and emotional disposition. He's got three options so predictable, so archetypal, that when I read it, I can't help but think about growing up with two older brothers. Wise, clever, and simple: That's us! We embody the same three temperaments that show up in stories and myths across cultures and throughout history. You can even find modern scientific studies about siblings that sometimes confirm and sometimes refute the impact of birth order — its bearing on success, achievement, intelligence, and confidence. Think of famous siblings in family movies and sitcoms; they often exhibit the same characteristics in the same order. Familiar patterns like these can be frighteningly persuasive, providing the persona masks that unconsciously shape our lives. Unfortunately, this is one of the ways we're nudged (or maybe, we unconsciously nudge ourselves) toward involuntarily living out scripts that reinforce narcissistic patriarchal authority.

To make this clear, let's get back to the story. The king intuitively understands that passing the crown is about choosing a new headspace, a new kind of consciousness for the entire kingdom, but this provokes anxiety for Dad. He can't make up his mind about which son exemplifies the right path. How could he? It's impossible. We all know the famous quote: "We can't solve problems by using the same thinking we used when we created them." These words are often misattributed to Albert Einstein, but he never said them; they're just folk wisdom, distributed through social media memes and fortified by the authoritative image of Einstein's brain.[20] Nonetheless, they express the inherent dilemma of a paradigmatic crisis well. What do you do when the former perspective crumbles and a new one must replace it? Methods, procedures, formulas, and criteria for solving these new puzzles haven't yet been established.[21] The problem *is* the problem-solving. So what does the king do? He leaves it to chance. He blows three feathers into the air and says, "As they fly, so shall you go."

It's augury—like flipping a coin, rolling dice, or spinning the roulette wheel. In our time, gambling is often seen as a sinful temptation, but games of chance have a long history of being associated with prophetic divination; they were once considered an empirical way to reveal the authoritative will of God. That's what happens in this story; the outcome is officially sanctioned by the holy father himself. As if by manifest destiny, one feather goes right, one feather goes left, and the third one falls to the ground. The wise brother and the clever brother head off in the direction of their feathers. The Dummling is distraught. "He sat down and was sad. Then all at once he saw that there was a trapdoor close by the feather."

Von Franz explains that the symbolism of the trapdoor is twofold. First, the Dummling is the only son humble and unsophisticated enough to discover the pathway hidden right in front of his nose. He doesn't have preconceptions or expectations about how things should go. He's not beholden to the old paradigm. He's not wise enough to be blinded by conformity. He's not clever enough to be looking for opportunities. His naiveté constitutes a kind of unencumbered autonomy similar to what Immanuel Kant described. Hence, he's well suited to earn the authoritative position on his father's throne. Second, because it's a passageway into the earth, von Franz says that it represents a journey into the depths of the unconscious. More important to us, she equates this underground space with "the feminine." Think: Mother Earth. The trapdoor exposes a tunnel down to a cavern of fertile gestation. Von Franz sees it as uterine symbolism. Something is about to be birthed.

To be clear, I usually take issue with the way Jungians use gender essentialism to describe psychological complexes. I cringe whenever I hear new-agey folks talk about divine feminine and masculine energy types. *Men penetrate, women encase. To be male is to enter and infiltrate, to be female is to hold and encompass.* It seems to me that cataloging these kinds of psychological inclinations or archetypal images according to gender just reinforces false assumptions about innate differences between *two* anatomical types—which not only strengthens the sexist foundation for misogynistic attitudes,[22] but also fails to acknowledge that a simple binary can't adequately represent the full spectrum of biological (or psychological) difference. Think about it this way: the trapdoor in "The Three Feathers" might indeed be a symbol of cognitive, creative, imaginative potential—the ability to innovate, to bring something new into existence. What's the benefit of thinking about these attributes as inherently feminine or masculine? I don't see one. However, in this case, I'll set my reservations aside because the story is from a time when gendered symbolism was the norm.

Notice that there's no queen in this story. That's pretty standard for fairy tales: there are lots of bad stepmoms and icy-cold evil queens, but not many good mothers. Why would they be involved? These are really stories about fathers and their narcissistic patriarchal authority, so Mom is irrelevant. In "The Three Feathers," there's not even a princess. All the significant characters are male. The reason, according to von Franz, is that it's a story about unhealthy masculine psychology. The kingdom is deteriorating because the so-called feminine aspects of the self are not well integrated. It's the same archetypal message that's at the core of the APA's *Guidelines for Psychological Practice with Boys and Men*. If von Franz wrote in contemporary terms, she might say the story is about how necessary it is for men to let go of the attitudes and behaviors associated with toxic masculinity. She might say men need to shed the hardened, defensive armor of manhood and embrace softer, gentler, and more vulnerable ways of being. Clearly, this is not rhetoric unique to the #MeToo era. Jungians were already talking about it in the mid-twentieth century, so why have we made so little progress? Maybe because then, as now, folks rarely take narcissistic patriarchal authority into account.

To do so, look at how the story concludes. The Dummling finds a bride at the end of the trapdoor tunnel. It's a small toad that turns into a beautiful woman. Von Franz sees toads as "Earth Mother" symbolism, a personification of the uterus.[23] But I think it might be more of that same amphibian, reptile-brain symbolism that informed my son's infant stroller! After all, a toad is a shapeshifter, a hybrid. Not only can it traverse aqua/terrestrial boundaries, but also it can change sex, it can turn over its chromosomes, presumably to maintain genetic and evolutionary continuity. Clearly, there's something about gender and sex here, but I don't agree with von Franz's take. She says the Dummling's union with his toad-bride represents a kingdom restored to its proper equanimity. From her perspective, the moral of the story is that a healthily individuated psyche balances masculine and feminine energies. I think the truth is way more sinister.

Of course, the idea of an unbalanced psyche restored to order through symbolic heterosexual coupling is common. Think of the most familiar princess fairy tales. They always end with a kiss, an engagement, or a wedding. Many critics have complained about these happily-ever-after endings, noting that Disney's princesses are completely defined by their desire to be saved by a handsome young prince. They have no agency or autonomy. I'm glad folks complain about this, but I don't think they're outraged enough. That's because they take the stories too literally. They see the princess as a distinct protagonist — a hero in her own incomplete and tragically oblique version of Joseph Campbell's monomyth — but that's not what she's meant to be. Instead, she's just one inner voice: one aspect of the self, a personified complex within the father-king's psyche, the monarch's kingdom. In that sense, she's nothing more than a prop in a misogynistic psychological allegory.

It's true that in "The Three Feathers," the toad-bride's entire purpose is to marry the Dummling, but von Franz gets one thing wrong. It's not a union; it's an acquisition. This is not true love; it's a financial investment. Back before the Brothers Grimm recorded the story — fixing it in its current form — a husband owned his wife and could even annul the arrangement if she didn't produce children. Her job was to make him a father. In other words, the story predates our modern romantic sensibilities. Today, ninety percent of wedded couples cite love and companionship as the motivation for getting married.[24] But as historian Stephanie Coontz explains, "Until the eighteenth century, most societies saw marriage as far too vital an economic and political institution to be left entirely to the free choice of individuals. Especially if they were going to base their decision on something as unreasoning and transitory as love."[25] The idea of a passionate connection between soul mates may be a common literary motif throughout history, but it wasn't considered something that happened between husband and wife until modern times. In the past, love had nothing to do with marriage. True love was considered catastrophic. Romeo and Juliet, Paris and Helen, Tristan and Isolde, Shah Jahan and Mumtaz Mahal, Alexander I of Serbia and Draga Mašin: history's paramours were tragically star-crossed precisely because passion got in the way of practical decision-making. Love was not a part of the recommended path toward happily ever after. Instead, the dowry was. Marriage contractually cemented your family's power, allegiance, property, and patrilineage. That was the key to contentment and social status.

So von Franz may be correct that the toad-bride bolsters the Dummling's capacity to inherit the kingdom, but their marriage is not a symbol of psychological individuation in the modern sense, and it's certainly not about respecting any qualities or characteristics culturally associated with women or femininity. It's about helping him become the father-king. He needed to own a uterus before he could rule the kingdom because nothing but patrilineage matters here. Everyone but the father figure is just a supplemental element in a narrative of narcissistic patriarchal authority. All things converge around Dad's needs, Dad's story, Dad's existence, and the continuity of Dad's patriarchal rule.

Is it any wonder then that fathers, raised on fairy tales, would see themselves as authoritative protagonists, entitled to determine the direction of their family's narrative? No. They're always imagined as the primary unit that organizes all of our lives. We may want to imagine our fathers as benevolent handymen — always fixing up and maintaining the love and sanctity of the homestead — but unfortunately, we can't just "make it so." We live in a patriarchal paradigm that expects Dad, as king and protagonist, to be the ultimate gaslighter.

Gaslights and Windmills

In the #MeToo era, we talk a lot about "gaslighting." That's a good thing, but it would be even better if we'd acknowledge how our unintentional reverence for paternal narcissism normalizes gaslighting and conditions us all to privilege authority over responsibility.

The term *gaslighting* is usually used to describe a form of psychological or emotional manipulation. It comes from a 1938 play called *Gas Light*. It's a story about a husband, Gregory, who tries to convince his wife, Paula, that she's going insane. He aims to have her hospitalized so that he can steal her jewels. He misplaces objects around the house and pretends that it's her fault that she can't find them. He regularly searches the attic for her valuables, and when he does, all the gaslights in the house dim. When Paula asks him about the dimming lights, Gregory tells her she's imagining things. Then, he suggests she needs to rest, because she's clearly not well.[26] His lies and distractions are the model for the behavior social scientists now call gaslighting.

In current usage, gaslighting rarely describes such extreme

examples of coercion. Instead, it refers to the way someone (not necessarily a cisgender man) takes control of an interpersonal narrative, destroying the victim's capacity to have a unique perspective, insisting that there's only one plausible version of a story.[27] *She's crazy. You're lying. It didn't happen that way!* University of Utah associate professor Cynthia A. Stark describes gaslighting as "testimonial injustice" because it denies the validity of an individual's "testimony about a harm or wrong done to her."[28] That's why the term is so often used in cases of sexual violence or abuse; a perpetrator does everything they can to suggest that their account of events is the only accurate one. Of course, gaslighting isn't always associated with abuse. There are many more common, everyday examples.

Gaslighting is everywhere. Most of the time — because the ability to author a narrative defines the way we think about agency — we inadvertently celebrate it as an indicator of autonomy. In fact, we expect it from fathers. We may not realize it, but each instance of narcissistic patriarchal authority reinforces the idea that paternal gaslighting is not only normal but also the only way in which one can be an effective father. Dad must "make it so." Combine this with hundreds if not thousands of folktales, bedtime stories, and myths that tell a symbolic story of psychological transformation that converges around a father or king — a Zeus-like protagonist — and, suddenly, it becomes clear that the capacity to enact a subtle kind of gaslighting permeates our conception of individual selfhood.

To see this problematic narrative of autonomy clearly, and to confront its implications, we'll need to understand how this unfortunate truth came to be. For that, we'll travel all the way back to the year 1637, when French philosopher René Descartes wrote his famous axiom, "I think, therefore I am" (*Cogito, ergo sum*).[29] It seems like everyone knows this phrase, but very few people really understand why it was so important to the "Age of Reason." Descartes was interested in a question that many of us have struggled with, especially in late-night existential conversations during our high school or college years. There's a good reason for this timing and it has little to do with the teenaged penchant for experimenting with inebriants. It's because adolescence is the crux of the Freudian duel for patriarchal status. It's when our hero's journey supposedly starts, when we begin to see ourselves as would-be father-figure gaslighters, as the potentially dominant authors of stories that can define the experience of our friends and loved ones.

The existential question that both Descartes and many adolescents grapple with is this: If everyone has their own subjective experience, why can't mine be the authoritative one? After all, how can we know for sure what's real? Is the world around us some sort of virtual simulation or a dream? Is my perception of color the same as yours? What constitutes opinion as opposed to fact? Is there ever such a thing as objectivity? Descartes had an answer to these questions. He said that the only thing we can know for sure is that our consciousness exists. I think, therefore I am. Everything else requires some sort of empirical investigation.

His solution seems obvious to us because we're all living in a post-Cartesian world, but it's hard to overstate just how revolutionary an idea *Cogito, ergo sum* was at the time. It characterized the era of modernity. Up until Descartes wrote his *Discourse on Method*, many philosophers had pondered the unreliability of human perception but nobody had successfully framed all of existence into an inner and outer world, an internal and an external reality. Often this concept is referred to as Descartes's "mind-body dualism," or sometimes "the Cartesian split." Why? Because it makes it possible for us to recognize the distinction between the physical brain — a tangible organ, a material part of the body composed of cells, synapses, and neurons — and the mind, an abstract entity that constitutes consciousness, sentience, and thought itself. From this dualistic perspective, the mind is within the brain. Therefore, the world can be divided into subjective and objective domains. The subjective domain is that private world of thoughts, observations, opinions, beliefs, and feelings with which we're all familiar. It's what we tend to think of as our "inner selves." It's where all our metaphorical princesses, toad-brides, and Dummlings reside — our own personal *Inside Out* control center. The objective domain is the external reality, which is made up of matter — things that can be measured, handled, and proven to exist as facts. Anything that can't be proven using the Cartesian scientific method should be considered a subjective fantasy or a delusion. Like the way Sir James Frazer defined Couvade syndrome: It's a "primitive" belief in sympathetic magic.

Most of us tend to accept this subject/object dualism without giving it a second thought. We believe in both an inner and an outer life. We take it for granted that reality needs to be empirically measurable. Consider the invisible yet omnipresent foundation for both neuroscience and psychology. A neuroscientist studies how the objective matter of the brain — cells, synapses, neurons — creates the subjective experience of the mind. A psychologist understands thinking, or cognition, as the process through which the mind constructs a subjective representation of the external, material, objective world. Both require Descartes's mind-body dualism.

Descartes gets the credit for inventing this outlook because we operate from within a patriarchal paradigm that favors individual authority — always framing a "great man" as the pivotal author of historic and philosophical change.[30] But the truth is, causality is rarely so independent. Plenty of other folks were already exploring the implications of this new way of being before Descartes described it. For instance, Miguel de Cervantes published *Don Quixote* just a few decades earlier in 1605. It's worth noting that Cervantes also benefits from the "great man" doctrine of history. That's why so many people consider *Don Quixote* to be the first modern novel. Why do they claim the book is so innovative? Because it's the story of a dualistic self, of the struggle between subjective (internal) and objective (external) realities.

Don Quixote is the tale of an old man who has read so many stories about great knights that he can't tell fact from fiction anymore. The Ingenious Gentleman of La Mancha now believes that he is a knight, and he misinterprets all the mundane aspects of his experience to be parts of an epic, heroic quest. The most famous scene in the book involves windmills. Don

Quixote and his squire, Sancho Panza, are riding through the countryside when they see thirty or forty windmills. Don Quixote thinks that they are "enormous giants" and announces his intention to do battle with them. Sancho objects: "Those things over there aren't giants, but windmills, and what looks like their arms are the sails that are turned by the wind and make the grindstone move." Don Quixote is not convinced.

"It seems clear to me," he says to Sancho, "that thou art not well versed in the matter of adventures: these are giants; and if thou art afraid, move aside and start to pray whilst I enter with them in fierce and unequal combat."[31]

He spurs his horse and charges. The wind begins to turn the sails, which just reinforces Don Quixote's conviction. Clearly, the giants began to move because they feared combat with such a great knight! The old man drives his lance into one of the sails and he's lifted into the air and thrown to the ground. Battered and bruised, he saunters away, but he does not abandon his delusion. He explains that some dark magic must have turned the giants into windmills, a clear effort by the forces of evil to impede his virtuous quest.

The novel is more than nine hundred pages of similar comedic episodes in which Don Quixote's subjective experience is in dispute with objective reality. Eventually, he does become a famous knight. Everywhere he goes, his reputation precedes him. People have heard about his delusional adventures, and although they know that he's not a true knight, they treat him as the heroic figure he imagines himself to be. The external world has been coerced into conforming with the internal story that Don Quixote authored. It's a perfect description of narcissistic patriarchal authority. He gaslighted everyone!

In a world that depends on Cartesian mind-body dualism to establish truth, knowledge, and meaning, we are all Don Quixote. Don't we share his strange blend of conviction and naiveté? We tend to know what we know well, but we don't even know enough to recognize the things we don't know. We like it that way; our self-worth and confidence — even our ability to wake up in the morning and perform the day's duties — are dependent on our capacity to remain blissfully unaware of our inherent contradictions. Like Don Quixote, we vigorously resist anything that threatens to dissolve the patchwork of narratives that drive the decisions we make and the actions we take. We'll gaslight our way right out of self-reflection. We'll tilt at windmills. In fact, we believe it's the right thing to do, the moral high ground. We even see it as the mark of competence and maturity. Survival of the fittest!

Consider that almost all self-help, psychology, and business development books frame personal agency and autonomy according to this capacity to "make it so." We consider the ability to narcissistically distort reality to be admirable. For example, Walter Isaacson interviewed Apple employees to learn how they perceived Steve Jobs. "The best way to describe the situation is a term from *Star Trek*," explained Bud Tribble, member of the original Macintosh development team. "Steve has a reality distortion field." Apparently, Jobs could persuade anyone to see a situation exactly the way he saw it, regardless of how delusional his view was. This caused programmers to commit to impossible delivery timelines. "It was dangerous to get caught in Steve's distortion field, but it was what led him to actually be able to change reality."[32] It sounds like Steve Jobs was Don Quixote — narcissistic, patriarchal, and authoritative to the core.

Similarly, whenever you hear people talk about manifesting better professional and/or health outcomes through positive thoughts, it's not just magical thinking; they are also caught up in narcissistic patriarchal authority. They may say: *Avoid negativity; Approach the world with gratitude; Believe in yourself and ignore the haters; Be the change you want to see; Miracles will happen!* It certainly sounds comforting and inspiring, but the new-age gurus and motivational speakers are all telling the same Cartesian, *Don Quixote* story. Few seem to realize that whenever we allow an individual's subjective fiction to define our collective, objective reality, we're also doubling down on a devotion to gaslighting.

In this way, we've all bought into the notion that one's capacity to employ narcissistic coercion is an indicator of success. It's especially true for fathers! They're living within a cultural paradigm that still considers Dad to be the primary unit of economic participation, the man of the house, the head of a *famulus*. Therefore, the call for reality distortion is implicit: Father knows best and the rest of us should conform to his testimony, his authorization, his version of reality. Whether he likes it or not, Dad is urged to embrace the mindset of "masculine" patriarchal authority. He's told the story should always belong to him. Mother and children are just supplemental, supporting characters in his heroic quest, but it doesn't have to be that way. A father figure can abandon his Don Quixote delusions. He can see alternatives to Descartes's mind-body dualism. He can avoid gaslighting. He can replace authority with responsibility.

Simply put, a feminist dad recognizes that we are all living in a network of mutual subjective realities; we're building a world of stories together.

Be Responsive

When my boys were little, I liked to drag the big plastic bin of wooden blocks to the center of the living room rug. The pieces inside were mixed shapes: cubes, cylinders, tetrahedrons, and spheres. Each one was sanded smooth and sealed with shellac to prevent splinters. I'd stack them into a royal tower — wide and stable at the foundation, but increasingly complicated and precarious as it rose toward the spinning ceiling fan overhead.

My self-issued challenge was to use every block, to balance them in the craziest, most haphazard positions. I took the ordeal very seriously, like it was the ultimate trial of father-hood heroism. The kids watched from the sidelines, on the edge of their seats, impatient and eager to play their parts. They'd hop up from the sofa the moment I placed the final cone, a crowning turret atop a masterwork of playful construction. Running on wobbly knees, the boys approached. Arms swinging like windmills, they knocked the whole thing down. *Boom!* The sound of the crash made them giggle; the mess delighted them even more. We'd laugh together, hug each other, and then I'd start all over again.

I think about that game often; I talk about it in my classes. It's a reminder that even a toddler can deconstruct things. The real skill lies in building them back up again. This is a parable to keep in mind as you develop the necessary critical consciousness to be a feminist dad. Always remember that it's much easier to call out the problematic narratives that shape our aspirations and expectations than it is to construct new ones. So much of feminist and intersectional theory does the important job of showing us how the ideas and structures we take for granted reinforce systemic inequality. Many brilliant manifestos have been written to encourage folks to recognize that patriarchal oppression maintains its stability because we continue to build our lives on a foundation of sexist presumptions. That's good; you must do that work first. You need to disassemble the scaffolding that upholds the ideological tyranny of what-goes-without-saying.[33] You have to break those old frameworks down. That's why hundreds of feminist books line my shelves, each one proffering tools for smashing familiar stories that normalize misogyny, homophobia, and transphobia. The problem is that very few of them offer a clear model for building back up, for writing better scripts. Maybe that's because there's an inherent enigma. How can you author a story, and recommend it to others, without succumbing to the delusional temptations of narcissistic patriarchal authority?

As activist adrienne maree brown writes, "We are socialized to see what is wrong, missing, off, to tear down the ideas of others and uplift our own."[34] It's true. We all argue, debate, and gaslight sometimes. Often these are just misguided attempts to maintain the stability of our own personal Don Quixote delusions. We try to offset fear and insecurity — to hide the symptoms of what people sometimes call "imposter syndrome."[35] Cisgendered men who live in imperialist white supremacist patriarchal capitalist societies are especially inclined toward these feelings of inadequacy and the odious defensive rhetoric that goes along with them.

It's not that we're being intentionally hateful, sexist, or racist. That is, you don't need to feel like a villain because 1) the story doesn't revolve around you and 2) you're probably not engaged in deliberate malice. Still, you're not without some culpability. After all, it's likely that you've been taught to imagine that growth and critical mass — attained through no-holds-barred, ends-justify-the-means competition — is the only way to achieve fulfillment and demonstrate status. You've been told it's connected to survival and evolutionary progress. Therefore, you mistake expansion as the defining attribute of positive transformation, and you also consider it an antecedent to revolutionary change. You build your tower of blocks as high as you can! Like a corporation trying to earn a bigger market share, or an Oedipal hero on a trajectory of murderous ascendancy, you're always looking for victory. Oftentimes, you need to push other people out of the way because wealth, power, and contentedness seem to depend on one's ability to be the primary author of a narrative amplified by a significantly large collective. It's tantamount to manspreading. You want your story to occupy more space. This kind of narrative seeding is the core objective promoted in a culture that holds media celebrity in such high regard. It's mirrored in our individual lives, especially now that so many of us are preoccupied with followers, comments, and likes. It's also at the root of many of the troublesome fathering behaviors associated with toxic masculinity. After all, it's no secret that dads dominate their families in order to magnify their own sense of importance — to bolster their narcissistic patriarchal authority. They bully where they can to compensate for shortcomings where they can't.

Of course, I'm not trying to imply that all dads are all bad all the time. I know that many fathers regularly acknowledge the importance of gender parity and call out misogyny whenever they see it. Sitting at the dinner table, discussing the school day, maybe they're diligent about correcting the gender stereotypes their kids pick up from their peers. Perhaps Dad is also careful to avoid using troublesome colloquialisms and vulgar idioms. For instance, he won't say: *You're a sissy; You throw like a girl; Take it like a man;* or *Grow a pair.* Likewise: *No slut shaming* and *Don't use words like* bitch *or* pussy. Some dads may go even further, intentionally challenging familiar gender roles by disrupting the common organization of household work. Who does all the cooking and cleaning in your home? Who washes and folds the laundry? Who pays the bills? Who handles power tools? Who schedules the doctor's appointments? Who arranges playdates and extracurriculars? The way you organize the routines of daily life is a structural model that your children will eventually incorporate into their understanding of what constitutes "normal." It can either confirm or challenge societal expectations, so make your choices mindfully.

When my kids were little, I went out of my way to point out sexist and homophobic representations on television and at the movies. I asked them to explain why all the female characters in their video games had such big boobs, why gay jokes were so prevalent in cartoons made for little kids. I also tried never to make heteronormative assumptions while talking to them. Imagining the future, I'd try to say things like, "I can't wait to embarrass you the first time you bring home a partner." I didn't say *girlfriend* because I didn't want to make heterosexual presumptions. I didn't even say *boyfriend* or *enbyfriend.* *(Enby* is a common phonetic pronunciation of the initials *N.B.,* as in *Non-Binary.)* I understood that any dreams I articulated about their future would set the standards and ideals for a lifetime of aspirations, and I didn't want them to feel limited by my expectations.

When we walked through Target or other big box retailers, I regularly made remarks about the absurdity of toys being divided into pink and blue aisles. What could possibly make a particular LEGO set more appealing to one gender than another? I asked my sons to explain it to me. Of course they couldn't, but I loved watching them struggle. One of my favorite pastimes was messing with my kids, confusing them in an attempt to provoke critical thinking. Sometimes other adults would give me sideways glances, or roll their eyes. They thought I was spoiling the children's fun. *Let them have their muscly superheroes and pink princesses; they like it, don't ruin it for them!* The implication was that little kids deserved a childhood free from social-justice concerns. I knew that was just plain wrong. Ubiquitous gender stereotypes are way more oppressive to a child's naiveté than any acknowledgment of misogyny, homophobia, or transphobia could ever be.

Nowadays, I often hear my boys challenging their friends' assumptions the same way I always challenged theirs. It makes me proud, but I recognize that these examples are not, in themselves, indicative of father-figure success. Being a feminist dad involves so much more than just making a commitment to avoiding sexist language and behaviors. It also involves changing your mindset — demolishing the attitudes and behaviors that inadvertently contribute to the very thing you've pledged to fight. In other words, you need to be less authoritative and more responsive.

What does that look like in practice? First of all, *responsive fathering* is participatory and adaptive. It's not about casting decisive thunderbolts; it's about witnessing and listening. That's why, now that my boys are teenagers, I'm constantly learning from them. I don't always like it: They regularly correct me when I use the wrong pronouns while referring to their friends. They also call me out for being inappropriately judgmental when I'm sharing anecdotes about my experience with students who were offended by something that happened during a classroom discussion. My initial reaction is almost always defensive. *I'm the expert. I taught you kids how to be feminists.*

You don't know more than me! But sometimes they do know more than me. I'm still learning that being the father figure doesn't mean I always get to have the last word.

The problem is that when you're stuck in the ego fallacy of narcissistic patriarchal authority, you think you're always entitled to "make it so"! But responsive fathering recognizes that reality is cocreated; it's collaborative and emergent. You need to listen to a variety of voices, without presuming that the loudest, most dominant represents a more accurate view. You need to apply this same hospitality whether you're welcoming internal or external voices. Whether you're listening to members of your family or engaged in self-reflection, the same process is required. In fact, a feminist dad can't do one without the other. Just as you need to respect the dignity and autonomy of your children and partners, you also need to trust that there's a variety of metaphorical *Inside Out* figures within your own psyche. Each one can bring a uniquely wise and sometimes unexpected perspective to any given situation. Which ones are you inadvertently silencing because your taken-for-granted assumptions harbor troublesome prejudices? Do some make you feel weak? Emasculated? Uncertain? Out of control? To figure that out, you need to listen to the discourse without overidentifying with one voice and pathologizing the others.

Remember, the solutions to your everyday dilemmas are never singular. That's an especially hard thing to acknowledge when you're stuck in the ego fallacy of narcissistic patriarchal authority. Why? Because you inadvertently subscribe to "the great man" theory of history — you assume that one individual voice can and will arrive at the best visionary answer to every paradigmatic problem. It doesn't stop with your admiration for Steve Jobs or your veneration of other celebrity icons and athletes. Chances are you also apply this concept to the daily vicissitudes of family life. You assume that "father knows best." Or at the very least, you believe that he should always be trying to know best. Hence, you're eager to offer paternal advice, to be a handyman who attacks problems with lightning-fast, thunderbolt solutions, but that's not responsive fathering. A feminist dad knows that real wisdom comes from cooperative intelligence — that an intersubjective and equitable truth manifests not only among equally respected human individuals, but also through the consensual discourse of internal psychological voices.

What would it look like for you to listen to all the voices in your home and in your head? What would it sound like when they coauthor a more mindful narrative? In the beginning of this chapter, I mentioned thundering silence. Thich Nhat Hanh writes, "To practice mindfulness of speech, sometimes we have to practice silence. Then we can look deeply to see what our views are and what internal knots give rise to our thinking."[36] This is good advice for feminist dads. It reminds me of my kids demolishing block towers. They did it with the expectation that the tower would be built back up and they could knock it down all over again. Likewise, the purpose of critical consciousness is to deconstruct the current cultural narratives in order to make space for newer, less-oppressive ones. But it's not a father figure's job to write the new story. Instead, a feminist dad releases the ego fallacy of narcissistic patriarchal authority and opens his ears so he can hear all the unique things being articulated in other people's stories.

PART THREE:

WHO'S YOUR DADDY?

FRIDAY, FEBRUARY 14, 4:17 P.M.: I know that a sugar high is not a real thing.[1] It's just bad science blended with urban legend. Victorian-era prudence was passed down, through old wives' tales, to early-twentieth-century doctors, who promoted restraint as a catchall cure to remedy children's bad behavior. Flawed research confirmed their bias: You are what you eat; practice temperance; overindulgence is a sin![2] Everyone believed it, and many still do, but the "sugar hypothesis" was never based on facts. Later studies consistently disproved the notion that sweets could impact behavior or cognition in negative ways.[3] That means the Twizzlers and Peppermint Patties are not making my kids hyperactive. My boys may indeed be loud and annoying, but they're probably just excited; we never have this much candy in the house. It's only here now because I opened the big box that my mother sent for Valentine's Day. She sends one every year. Her father always sent one for her, and now she continues the tradition.

Grandpa lived in Lakewood, New Jersey. He sent the candy by mail to Philadelphia. There was no online shopping in those days, so every hand-addressed, kraft-paper-covered package was still cause for excitement. This one, especially so. My brothers and I tore the plastic shrink-wrap from the giant red heart-shaped carton. We opened it as if a revelation were waiting inside. Instead, we found a mystery. There was no guide, nothing printed on the inside of the box top, no way to identify the flavor of each bite-sized confection, but that was half the appeal. We entered a fierce competition to see who could better guess which was a caramel turtle, a dark ganache truffle, or a gooey marshmallow chew. Nobody wanted the jellies.

Today, my mom has swapped out the old heart box for multiple bags of mass-produced Halloween favorites. My pantry is overflowing with Haribo Goldbears, Milky Way bars, and Reese's Pieces. My boys are annoyed that I keep reminiscing about the golden years of real chocolate gift boxes. They just don't care; they respond to Grandma's care package with the same mindless vigor that my brothers and I once felt about our grandpa's.

I suppose it's nice that this tradition has traversed generations, but the truth is, it always confused me. Why would a father send a Valentine's Day gift to his daughter? Why would a mother send one to her son? Isn't the holiday about a different kind of love? We called it "like-like" when I was in middle school. *Do you like her? Or do you like-like her?* That's how we distinguished between a wannabe girlfriend and a friend who was a girl. Like the ancient Greek philosophers, my pubescent friends and I were differentiating *philia* (φιλία) from *eros* (ἔρως) — two distinct kinds of love.

I always think of philia as "brotherly love." It's because I'm from Philly, and that's what it's known as: the city of brotherly love. It's not exactly an accurate translation. Philia is not exclusive to siblings — who also don't always have amorous relationships. To be more precise: The Greek word refers to the love between folks who share a common bond. Biological kinship is just one example. Business partners and countrymen are other possibilities. Aristotle applied the term *philia* to any friendships motivated by goodwill, utility, or simple pleasures.[4] In contrast, eros is lustful. It describes the kind of love that typically leads to romance and sex. It's a deep, probing desire.[5] But in middle school, even our like-like wasn't erotic in that sense. Having a girlfriend was mostly a status thing. We were trying to fit in. We didn't hook up or make out. Mostly we just sat together, awkwardly, on the bus or at a lunch table in the cafeteria. Maybe we held hands at recess while all the kids blathered about who like-liked whom.

It would be a few years before we started petting and grinding. By then, a lot of the guys said that it was impossible for a boy to have a friend who was a girl. Using exceptionally crude words and phrases, they argued that eros would always get in the way. At first I didn't believe them. I had plenty of friends who were girls, many of whom I had never thought about in romantic ways, but once the pubescent gossip mill taught me to interpret my hormonal affect according to binary social conventions, I began to wonder: If a female friend's interest in me were sexual, would my interest automatically become sexual, too? Are boys just built that way — always horny, always trying to "get some"? Innately promiscuous? Sexually assertive? Predatory like cavemen? There were so many so-called facts about the sexes that middle-school boys expounded on when the girls weren't around. Somebody had learned something from an older brother, or maybe a lewd uncle, and they parroted it with unrelenting conviction. They also ridiculed anyone who looked surprised or skeptical; the humiliation deterred dissent. Soon the lies, misconceptions, and fabrications of the pubescent imagination felt incontrovertible. Valentine's Day was transformed in my mind from a low-stakes exchange of chalky, candy-conversation-hearts and licensed cartoon greeting cards, to a high-pressure adolescent courting and mating ritual. All the cultural messaging had made it crystal clear: Valentine's Day was about eros, not philia.

And yet Grandpa, who had only the purest intentions, kept sending chocolates to my mom. Why? Because their relationship was influenced by a problematic reinterpretation of Freud's Oedipus complex — a way of thinking about dads, daughters, and adolescence that emerged in the 1940s. As you'll soon see, there's a lot we take for granted about how fathers engage with their daughters that's loaded with troublesome heteronormative presumptions about eros, gender, and sex. We've bought into some disturbing, misogynistic beliefs. We've put biological determinism at the core of our thinking around female sexual development, and we've baked it right into the facile expectations of father-figure identity. Being a feminist dad requires confronting the sordid, uncomfortable history of daddy–daughter relationships and abandoning the fallacies of locker-room gender essentialism.

Locker-room gender essentialism is a catchall phrase that I use to identify common narratives suggesting that attitudes around sex and intimacy are biologically determined — that boys are inherently one way and girls another, that penises and vaginas are uniquely associated with certain behavioral inclinations. When I was an adolescent, anecdotes claiming to unravel the mysteries of the vagina were shared like gospel in the boys' locker room. These fallacies became deeply integrated into my worldview. I was already middle-aged before I recognized that my middle-school assumptions were false — not least of all because there's no scientific basis for the sociocultural gender binary nor the anatomical genital binary. Nonetheless, locker-room gender essentialism continues to influence almost everyone. It not only contours the way daddies interact with their little girls but also determines a shockingly substantial number of our fatherhood habits of mind. It shapes our dad personas, defining the ways we expect a father figure to participate in the nuclear family. It guides many of our seemingly mundane and superficial actions. Therefore, even dads with the best intentions continue to reinforce wrongheaded heteronormative and binary ideas.

To be a feminist dad, you'll need to recognize how these

outdated ways of thinking continue to impact our everyday parental inclinations and our family routines. So often, we're inadvertently sending our children the worst possible messages about gender, sex, intimacy, and family dynamics.

She's Got Daddy Issues

Trends in psychology are always shifting. New ideas about best practices in childcare pop up all the time, just as often as old ones go out of vogue. Nutrition, education, sleep, exercise, screen time: Everything is fodder for parenting experts.

It's fair to assume that novel child-rearing customs gain traction only when they seem well intentioned — when folks expect that fresh ideas in child development will lead to progress, to better social and emotional outcomes. Often, in retrospect, what once seemed "evolved" can look scandalously regressive. One such theory became popular around the mid-twentieth century.

Folks in the United States were sure that they had figured out — once and for all — a scientific truth about psychological development: A father figure was at the center of a girl's adolescent transformation. It was a shockingly explicit example of narcissistic patriarchal authority. Doctors, psychiatrists, movies, and magazine articles all told Dad that he played the primary role in his daughter's sexual awakening. This misguided assumption has had a long-lasting and troublesome impact on all of us. It has shaped some of our taken-for-granted assumptions about sex, gender, and consent. It has amplified problematic conjectures, reinforcing delusions of gender essentialism, and it has distorted the way dads think about father-figure identity. To be a feminist dad, you need to understand this history. You also need to reflect on how your current attitudes remain anchored in a problematic past. Then you need to reimagine your dad persona so that it's better attuned to the possibility of a post-patriarchal future.

Start by confronting the past. During the 1940s and '50s, a new teen-centric adaptation of Freud's theory of infantile sexuality was endorsed both by most psychologists (not just men) and by most of the authors and practitioners who shaped common attitudes and prescribed best practices for child-rearing.[6] The experts all agreed that the way a father witnesses his daughter blossoming into a mature woman is the defining factor in her sexual development. Her well-being was supposedly dependent on how well he responded to this second edition of her Oedipus complex.[7]

Remember, in part one I explained how Freud's Oedipus complex is based on Sophocles's play *Oedipus Tyrannus*. It's the tale of a boy who's destined to marry his mother and kill his father. Freud reframed the mythological story as a symbolic representation of a universal stage in child development. At three to five years old, he said, a child has unconscious sexual attraction to the opposite-sex parent, and unconscious aggression directed toward the same-sex parent. The stage ends when the child begins to identify with the same-sex parent and repress the sexual instincts. Freud considered it a formative part of an individual's psychological development—and in that sense, memories of a traumatic Oedipal experience can contribute to the neuroses of teenagers and adults—but the actual Oedipal stage was presumed to be over long before puberty.

In the mid-twentieth century, after Freud died, psychoanalysts adopted a different perspective. They came to view adolescence as a second Oedipal stage, specifically impacting the developmental process through which a girl matures into a woman. They believed that the way a father responds to his daughter's unconscious attraction ultimately determines her social, emotional, and sexual well-being. Simply put, if Dad gives her too much attention, she'll never be satisfied with another man; she'll become permanently fixated on her father. If he gives her too little, she'll become sexually promiscuous, always seeking the validation that wasn't provided; she'll have daddy issues. The father–daughter relationship became an oddly eroticized balancing act.

"He was amused when she tried on her first pair of high heels, astounded when she appeared in her first cocktail dress, and weak-kneed when she emerged for her first junior prom," writes Rutgers University history professor Rachel Devlin. She's characterizing the common and popular cultural expectations for being a good dad during the 1940s and '50s.[8] At that time, the remnants of Victorian-era prudishness had fallen out of fashion and the United States was on the cusp of a sexual revolution. It would take more than a decade for second-wave feminism to really gain momentum, but there was already a fresh openness to thinking empathetically about the psychosexual lives of women. There was also a new level of awareness turned toward the experience of adolescent girls.

Helen Valentine launched *Seventeen* magazine in 1944 and its first run of four hundred thousand copies sold out in just a few days. The modern teenage girl — dubbed "Teena" in the promotional materials used to attract advertisers — became an uber-valuable consumer demographic. One direct mailing introduced Teena as the high school girl who "influences the buying habits of her family, chooses the clothes she wears, the lipstick she uses, the food she eats."[9] Retailers saw a huge market opportunity. They were eager to meet Teena's needs, but they also recognized that any money she wanted to spend would ultimately need to be coaxed from her breadwinner father. That's okay, she was up to the challenge: "Our girl Teena won't take no for an answer when she sees what she wants in *Seventeen*."[10]

Some scholars have argued that the magazine's consumer advertising created the adolescent-girl ideal that we now take for granted — the image we see in high-school sitcoms and teen movies.[11] A few folks have written about how *Seventeen* also played a part in transforming the father figure from an overbearing and authoritarian guardian of chastity to a liberal supporter of his daughter's emerging sexual independence. This shift was widely reflected in pop culture, where Dad was now depicted as the big-hearted comptroller of his teenage girl's impressive spending power. Many advertisements at the time depicted him helping his princess choose her look — sweaters, makeup, jewelry. Clearly, he adored her and wanted to make her happy, so self-help literature and advice columns encouraged Daddy and daughter to shop together, framing it as a perfect bonding experience. He was told he should comment on her appearance in ways that made her feel beautiful, worthy, and confident.

On the surface, Dad was offering his subjective evaluation of her clothing and cosmetic choices, but from a psychological development perspective, he was also taking a complicit and facilitative role in her presentation of sexual allure. By indulging or forbidding her purchases, Dad was witnessing and enabling his daughter's transformation into a mature, well-coiffed, beautiful woman. He was helping her learn how to tell a new story, and, no doubt, his feedback influenced her identity narrative. Therefore, he needed to do it well — offer approval in ways that made her feel confident but not boastful, attractive but not licentious, autonomous but not uninhibited.

To do so, the experts all agreed — and they were explicit about it — Dad should imagine himself as his adolescent daughter's first boyfriend. It wasn't supposed to be incestuous.[12] It was about routines and episodes that were lightly tinged with symbolic eros. As Rachel Devlin explains, "the walk down the aisle, the first dance at the coming-out party, [and] the presentation of gifts" are rites of passage that emphasize that "girls should (and inevitably would) look to their fathers, before anyone else, for sexual approval."[13] The message was clear: Dad should be the model for the man a woman eventually chose to marry.

Perhaps you're convinced that we've already moved away

from this disturbing way of thinking. We haven't. It still characterizes our assumptions about what it means to be a father figure. Consider this oft-quoted line from Sarah Ruhl's 2003 play *Eurydice*: "A wedding is for daughters and fathers. The mothers all dress up, trying to look like young women. But a wedding is for a father and daughter. They stop being married to each other on that day."[14] Or this statement from bestselling devotional author Gregory Lang: "A daughter needs a dad to be the standard against which she will judge all men."[15] Or how about this sentiment, attributed to Lady Gaga? "I love my daddy. My daddy's everything. I hope I can find a man that will treat me as good as my dad." These are all considered inspirational quotes that grace innumerable social media memes, especially those posted around Father's Day — which anecdotally suggests that they validate and reinforce people's existing expectations for fathers. These are current feel-good messages, supposedly aspirational and inspiring statements about what it means to be a good dad.

Likewise, just about every newspaper advice column and online blog-listicle about how dads should interact with their daughters includes remnants of the symbolically erotic daddy–daughter bond. Otherwise good advice about how dads can help encourage girl power and self-confidence becomes troublesome as soon as it's framed as a way to shape a woman's expectations for future romantic relationships. Think about it this way: It's true that you should be careful not to discourage your daughter's anger because it's so easy to reinforce the cultural messaging that calls assertive or aggressive women unfeminine, nasty, or bitchy — you don't want to teach her that good women should be content and complacent all the time. It's also true that you should compliment her intellect, her strength, and her competence rather than her appearance. The problem is that good pieces of advice like these are often ruined by the implication that they're about modeling future partnership expectations. For instance, I'll often hear dads tell their daughters, "Find a husband who treats you even better than I do." No! That's wrong. Instead, expect every man, woman, or other gender-nonconforming individual — in every situation — to treat you with honor and respect. Dignity is not just for lovers.

Unfortunately, the remnants of this Oedipal Stage 2.0 thinking don't linger just on social media or in popular advice columns; many experts still think this way, too. For instance, when I was in graduate school during the early 2010s, one professor lectured on the essential, archetypal psychology of girls. She told us stories about how Zeus adores his daughter Athena. One example: At the beginning of the *Odyssey*, Athena begs her daddy to release Odysseus from Poseidon's furious interference, to let the hero return to Ithaca. Homer describes Athena as "bright-eyed" and "beguiling."[16] I imagine she bats her lashes and shuffles her feet coyly — the way a clichéd character in a family sitcom begs her dad for a credit card, or car keys, or to overrule the strict curfew that Mom put in place. She's stereotypically conniving, using symbolic sexual allure as an instrument of manipulation. Read from a twenty-first-century perspective, Athena looks just like Teena, and, of course — like a TV dad — Zeus seems more than happy to oblige. He can't resist his little girl's charms! The brilliant, revered Jungian analyst standing at the front of my graduate school seminar explained that when it comes to adolescent girls, the paternal challenge involves navigating a tricky boundary. Teach her to toe the line between altruistic caretaker and femme fatale. The implication is that a father figure needs to be mindful about how he responds to his daughter's entreaties because it establishes her adult approach to wielding erotic power transactionally.

There are so many things that are problematic about this psychological schema once you unpack it just a little bit. For instance, it's a recklessly binary and heteronormative way of thinking. It not only assumes an innate Oedipal attraction between a child and their opposite-sex parent but also frames that attraction as the singular defining element in a girl's healthy adolescent development. Does that mean a child of same-sex parents is hopelessly doomed because there's not an appropriately gendered symbolic sexual object, i.e., no dad? Does that mean gender-nonconforming individuals — parents or children — automatically spoil the process of healthy child development? Both notions are certainly implicit in at least one argument that is often used in opposition to LGBTQ+ marriage equality: *A girl needs a father figure!* But all the research shows that it's an invalid concern.

There may be specific kinds of child–parent interactions that are necessary for healthy development, but they are absolutely not dependent on the sex or gender of the parent. That should be obvious. Why? Because as you know, the nuclear family, in the form we currently imagine it — with its gendered parenting roles — didn't even become the standard until the Industrial Age. Polygamy and cooperative breeding were normal once, too.[17] As were a plethora of other family arrangements, so it's absurd to think that emotional well-being is objectively dependent on conforming to a family structure that's only been fashionable for the last few generations. If it were, every human female who came of age prior to the eighteenth century would've suffered from devastating sexual neuroses. They didn't.

Your Prototypical Boyfriend

Chimamanda Ngozi Adichie writes, "Love is not only to give but also to take. This is important because we give girls subtle cues about their lives — we teach girls that a large capacity of their ability to love is their ability to sacrifice their selves."[18] I'd argue it's even worse than Adichie suggests.

The expectation that a paternal authority figure be the model for a girl's future romantic relationships masquerades as a good-natured and psychologically grounded strategy for fighting gender inequality, counteracting misogynistic messaging, and building better aspirations for womanhood. Meanwhile, it cunningly reinforces the same old patriarchal expectation that women be complacent and obedient. Clearly, if Dad is seen as the prototypical boyfriend, then a skewed power dynamic with a future partner is implicit. After all, a father is never his daughter's equal. He's an authority figure. Plus, her survival and well-being are completely dependent on him — or at least it feels that way to her. Pretending otherwise is tantamount to gaslighting; it's a Don Quixote delusion that multiple generations of dads have accepted without question.

In the 1940s and '50s, the erotic daddy–daughter relationship was framed as a modern, progressive, and empathetic acceptance of teen-girl independence—and in that sense it appealed to compassionate fathers, like my grandpa, who wanted their daughters to become strong, confident, independent women, like my mother, but every box of candy hid a covert form of consumption-oriented patriarchal authority. Girls learned that love, attraction, and respect are things you earn in the eyes of an authority figure— that dignity and worth are like merit badges you secure in exchange for demonstrating proper appearances and behaviors.

To understand why so many people bought into this narrative, and how a feminist dad can counteract it, first you need to recognize how Oedipal Stage 2.0 fits into a historical shift toward a seemingly democratic organization of family life. Many scholars have observed that the relationship between parents and their children became increasingly egalitarian around the mid-twentieth century. As authors Sonia Livingstone and Alicia Blum-Ross put it, parents became "accountable to their children in a relationship founded ever less on asserting authority and ever more on building mutual respect."[19] Family life was now negotiated. The father was no longer seen as a heavy-handed shepherd who should corral his daughter toward proper individualization. Instead, as sociologist Ulrich Beck argued, children "individualize *themselves*."[20]

Beck calls this the "biographization" of youth. What he means is that people started to see childhood as a process of learning to write your own story. You discover agency through milestone events like a first kiss, a driver's license, a prom date. You struggle to "find yourself." Within this framework, the role of the parent supposedly becomes less about steering or governing, and more about encouraging and supporting a child as they construct a narrative that's unique, individual, and self-authored. Agnes Callard, University of Chicago associate professor of philosophy and prolific blogger, frames it as a shift from "traditional parenting" to "acceptance parenting." She points out that *tradition* comes from the Latin verb *trādere*, meaning "to hand over." She writes, "If I were a traditional parent, I would be trying to give my child some version of *my* life; as an acceptance parent, I am trying to give my child something I don't have and am not familiar with."[21] At first glance, you'd think this change signifies a move away from narcissistic patriarchal authority, but when you look a little closer, you realize that—at least when it comes to fathers and their daughters—it's a tricky and duplicitous story.

Notice that this shift in family dynamics coincides with the rise of a media-driven consumption economy. That's not an accident. Biographization is achieved through self-presentation.[22] And in a capitalist marketplace, it involves purchasing material goods. Think back to the explanation of Erving Goffman's theory of the performing self that I offered in part one. He used theater as his metaphor. He said the self, as we know it, is created in response to its social context. In other words, we're all performers responding to the feedback we receive from our audiences. An actor on the stage of life requires costumes and props, so each crop top, mani-pedi, tube of lipstick, record album, and expensive haircut is an opportunity for self-expression, to tell your story. No wonder the advertising in *Seventeen* was so effective. It not only appealed to Teena, but also allowed Dad to maintain his patriarchal dominance within an increasingly egalitarian household. He could participate in seemingly open family negotiations while surreptitiously controlling his daughter's choices. He could communicate approval and condemnation—enmeshed with eros and sexual allure— through symbolic acts of deprivation or indulgence.[23] Therefore he could still wield his breadwinner authority while acting like a feminist. He could cast the deciding vote on every aspect of his daughter's biography by paying for what he liked and refusing to dole out cash for the rest. He maintained his chief executive status even while encouraging her personal narrative of liberated agency.

It paints a dark and disturbing picture. The daddy–daughter relationship looks like a transactional erotic hierarchy on which a girl's self-worth depends—which makes it even more troubling that girls are told to act out the same role in all future romantic endeavors. Maybe this sheds some light on why a 2018 study by UBS Global Wealth Management found that seventy-one percent of women in opposite-sex marriages believe their husbands should be responsible for providing them with a sense of financial security, and eighty-seven percent of husbands said they expected to do so. Could it be that the tangled bond between a father's financial authority and his daughter's sexual allure has been reproduced in adulthood? For grown-ups, it becomes: patriarchal husband and his metaphorically indentured wife, now masquerading as coequal spouses. It's even more worrisome to consider that these attitudes aren't limited to folks who came of age in the 1940s and '50s. The same views hold even among millennials. Sixty-one percent of these young women said they defer to their husbands on financial decision-making; that's more than Gen X (fifty-five percent) or Boomers (fifty-four percent).[24] As Harvard sociology professor Alexandra Killewald told the *New York Times* in 2018, "We have held on to the idea that men are supposed to provide, but have loosened up on the idea that women have to be homemakers."[25] Even in the #MeToo era, the 1950s' narrative of transactional daddy–daughter eroticism seems to be alive and well. It's just hiding in the shadows.

That's why a feminist dad needs to acknowledge that even when he's trying his best, it's possible for old misogynistic narratives to affect not only the way he chooses his own father-figure persona, but also the way he performs parenting practices and relates to his children. Consider that even the best fatherly intentions might harbor distorted cues that inadvertently reinforce patriarchal power dynamics. On the surface, everything may feel and look all right. Dad's trying his best, doing everything he can to cultivate confident, well-adjusted children. He embraces the idea of a more democratic family dynamic. He recognizes that it is in his children's best interest for him to eliminate father-knows-best, thunderbolt authoritarianism from his repertoire, but that's not enough. It takes more than that to be a feminist dad. It also requires staying skeptical, being on your guard, and engaging the instruments of critical consciousness. If you're not exceptionally mindful of the ways in which you negotiate with your children, you may replicate the same sexist identity narratives you're trying to fight.

Especially when it comes to daughters, a feminist dad needs to ask: How do I support her process of biographization without reinforcing the heteronormative and binary inequities that Oedipal Stage 2.0 thinking takes for granted? And to complicate things even more, you need to do that while shunning narcissistic patriarchal authority. In other words, you need to nurture her capacity for autonomous persona staging while simultaneously keeping your own father/king fairy tale out of the limelight. The key is responsive fathering. You need to recognize that you and your daughter are mutually engaged in a process of co-biographization. You need to allow your narrative of father-figure identity to be shaped by her, just as much as her adolescent identity narrative will inevitably be shaped by you.

This became clear to me the first time I heard the phrase "colliding myths." It was when I was thirty years old, just after my younger son was born, immediately following the depressive episode I described in part one. I was in therapy, seeing a Jungian analyst multiple times per week. At that time, much of my anxiety and emotional angst was the result of discovering that many of the life choices I had made were out of alignment with the image I held of myself and the father-figure persona mask I tried to display to my children. Therefore, most of my analytic sessions involved reflecting on stories from childhood. That means I spent a lot of time whining and complaining about my parents and my older brothers. I didn't feel seen by them. I felt invisible, like they always refused to acknowledge that my experiences deviated from theirs. One day, after a particularly self-serving rant, my analyst looked at me, tilted her head to one side, and matter-of-factly said, "Well, we're all living in colliding myths, so I don't understand why you would expect them to see you as the hero when that's obviously not your role in any of their stories." That blew my mind, and it completely changed the way I interacted with everyone in my life, especially my sons. It made me realize that a truly democratic family dynamic is a dizzying, chaotic tangle of mutual and contradictory biographies.

Full disclosure: I don't have daughters. That is, I don't have children who identify as girls. I acknowledge — as all feminist dads should — that it's a lot easier for those who identify as boys to receive the message that their process of autonomous biographization is valid than it is for those who identify as girls to receive the message. All the cultural coding is constantly reinforcing the idea that boys will one day be entitled to narcissistic patriarchal authority. For girls, however, the opposite is true. Most of what they see on television, on the internet, and in advertising is telling them that their stories should be defined by the men in their lives. That's why fathers need to make an intentional effort to counteract the covert consumer messaging of Oedipal Stage 2.0. How do you do it? By listening carefully to the stories your children are telling, not only through their words but also through their actions. Remember, you're not the judge nor the benefactor, so don't try to fix things; their identities are not flat tires, leaky faucets, or overdrawn checking accounts. Just listen, witness, and let them know that (in most cases) you're willing to engage with the fairy tale in precisely the way they're describing it — so much so that you'll change your own story to make it resonate with theirs.

Somebody's Daughter

How many times have you heard someone say that all men should be feminists because every woman is somebody's daughter? It seems like whenever there's high-profile, mainstream media coverage about sexual iniquity toward a famous woman, comments and memes flood the internet. *Imagine if she were your mom. Would you want someone to treat your sister that way? She's somebody's daughter!* At first glance, the comparison may look like a reasonable way to evoke understanding and empathy. After all, we assume that ideas are easier to grasp when contextualized in ways that communicate immediate personal relevance, but it's not always true. You can't take "the empathy altruism hypothesis" for granted.[26]

The empathy altruism hypothesis is a concept originally articulated by psychologist C. Daniel Batson. It describes the presumption that empathy is always good because, supposedly, being able to imagine how somebody feels will automatically trigger compassion, proactive concern, and a desire to help. Most of us take this for granted; we equate empathy with kindness, but research has repeatedly shown that empathy doesn't always correlate with altruism. For example, one neuroimaging study discovered that Red Sox and Yankees fans feel sadness when their own team strikes out, but experience pleasure while imagining the disappointment rival fans might feel in response to their own team's failure. Both are empathetic reactions. One is compassionate, the other is what's often called schadenfreude — the pleasure one derives from witnessing or imagining another person's misfortune.[27] Folks are more likely to experience the altruistic kind of empathy for loved ones or members of their own community — those with whom they have a philia bond. So a father may be magnanimously empathetic to his own daughter — maybe even to women who remind him of his daughter — but he may still be a misogynist jerk in every other context.

Obviously, being a feminist dad has little to do with loving your daughter — or even having empathy for people whom you consider in the same category as your daughter. Instead, you need to be committed to ending oppression, exploitation, inequality, and all other forms of social injustice. There's no reason to assume that having a daughter nudges you in that direction. In fact, there's evidence that some fathers double down on patriarchal dominance and authority precisely because they love their little girls. Studies have shown that fathering daughters can make some men more likely to adopt conservative stances on gender-related political issues like abortion, teen sex, and affirmative action.[28] Presumably, these fathers cling to old notions of women's propriety and paternal protectionism. Dad becomes more territorial, more controlling, more patriarchal — as if his job, in a dog-eat-dog world, is to guard his women from the vicious threat of other men. Maybe he believes he's conforming to an evolutionary script. *Be custodial; your reptilian-brain instincts compel you to protect your patrilineal estate!* Of course, this is not true. It's just another attempt to use locker-room gender essentialism to substantiate systemic misogyny.

A few studies have found that having daughters does cause some men to exhibit more liberal political attitudes. Adam N. Glynn at Emory University and Maya Sen at Harvard University compared the family composition of 224 U.S. Courts of Appeals judges against the results of nearly one thousand gender-related cases that those judges decided — cases that had "gender," "pregnancy," or "sex" in the LexisNexis case classification headings. Glynn and Sen found that "judges with daughters consistently vote in a more feminist fashion on gender issues than judges who only have sons."[29] But these results are hardly conclusive. Another study, done in 2018 by Elizabeth A. Sharrow and her colleagues at the University of Massachusetts, found that a father's support for sex-equity policies depends on whether the daughter is the *first* child. They called it the "First-Daughter Effect." Regardless of age or existing political affiliation, dads were more likely to support feminist policies if their firstborn identified as female. Neither having a daughter in general nor fathering more daughters had the same effect.[30]

What can we deduce from all these contradictory results? Not much. There's no clear empirical evidence to support the idea that fathers change their perspective, toward or away from feminism, because of their daughters.

Yet many men believe they do become more empathetic to women's issues after they have daughters. That's what the #GirlDad hashtag that blew up on Twitter in early 2020 was trying to insinuate. People interpreted it in exactly that way, congratulating the folks who tweeted about their little princesses. Can you blame them? The father–daughter effect is a common assumption, one of those things that many of us take for granted. Think of how often we hear comments from celebrity womanizers and pickup artists; they express regret about their old attitudes now that they've become a #GirlDad. Maybe it's a popular musician who previously recorded violent, disrespectful lyrics about sexual conquest. Maybe it's a comedian whose act once depended on sexist and misogynist stereotypes. As soon as they have daughters, they say that they feel remorse about their old rhetoric and behaviors. Now they've had a great feminist awakening! But it seems like what they're really worried about, in most cases, is that their beloved daughter might be treated as prey by men who are "innately predisposed" to being sexual aggressors. No doubt it makes for an entertaining sound bite on a late-night talk show, but the truth is that this kind of paternal protectionism is really just another manifestation of locker-room gender essentialism, which only serves to reinforce the patriarchal status quo.

Consider a couple more examples. Author Kyl Myers,

describing the challenges involved in choosing clothing for a gender-neutral toddler, complains about onesies and T-shirts with sexualized phrases like "Lock Up Your Daughters" or "Daddy Says No Dating Till I'm 40."[31] The same sentiment is echoed in the jokes you'll often hear from new dads. One father told me, "The first time a boy comes to take my daughter out on a date, I'll hang his 'nads from the door as a warning to the others." These sentiments masquerade as custodial, protectionist love, but they have nothing to do with being a feminist dad. Instead, they perpetuate fallacies of biological determinism. The truth is that those who identify (or are biologically assigned) as boys are not innately hornier, nor naturally more inclined toward reckless sexual behavior, than those who identify (or are biologically assigned) as girls. Even if they were, it wouldn't be a dad's job to monitor his daughter's sexual choices. Her body is not his property. Certainly, all parents bear responsibility for raising confident children who can make informed decisions about consensual sexual behavior. But if you really think your daughter is so dainty that she loses her autonomy and good judgment when she's alone with her partner — if you think she'll be flushed and exasperated by strange and confusing physical sensations — you've probably already failed.

The point is: A father's desire to preserve his daughter's sexual purity is the furthest thing from feminism. As is the notion that a #GirlDad's newfound repugnance for pickup artists is somehow anti-patriarchal. A father may indeed want people to treat his daughter with respect and dignity, but that doesn't necessarily tell us anything about his standpoint on women in general. Kate Manne frames this idea exceptionally well in her 2017 book, *Down Girl: The Logic of Misogyny*. She does it by drawing an important distinction between sexism and misogyny: "Sexism wears a lab coat; misogyny goes on witch hunts." What she means is that sexism has to do with ideology. It tries to justify inequality by asserting that there are inherent differences between sexes, so it's sexist when somebody argues that men and women are each naturally inclined toward certain societal roles, or that they're predisposed to specific sexual behaviors. Whenever we abide the fallacies of biological determinism, it implies that the fight against imbalance or discrimination is ultimately futile — that inequality is just the way things have always been, the way they're supposed to be.

In contrast to sexism, Manne says misogyny has to do with "enforcing" and "policing." It manifests as actions, speech, and attitudes that maintain and fortify cisgendered men's privileged positions of power. The word *misogyny* literally means to hate women. It combines the Greek μισο (*miso*), meaning "hate," with γυνή (*gyna*), meaning "woman" or "female." As Manne explains, misogynists "need not hate women universally, or even very generally."[32] You can love your daughter, her friends, and her basketball teammates.[33] You can hire women and believe that they are competent individuals.[34] But it's still misogynist if you hate outspoken women or feminist political ideas — because you're really objecting to potential disruptions of the patriarchal status quo.

You need to keep this distinction in mind if you want to be a feminist dad. You must recognize that it's easy for a father to believe that his daughter deserves equality even as he clings to many of the sexist assumptions of locker-room gender essentialism. Likewise, when it comes to misogynistic power structures, a father may want his daughter to feel free and empowered, but he still polices her behavior in ways that maintain his own narcissistic patriarchal authority.

The somebody's-daughter analogy is clearly faulty. At best it's naïve, self-congratulatory, and sentimental. At worst it's another example of narcissistic patriarchal authority (a woman's worth shouldn't be tied to her relationship with a man; we should recognize that she's someone, not just someone's daughter). Either way, one thing is clear: There's no reason to associate paternal love with feminist inclinations. If anything, the opposite assumption — that Dad would be both sexist and misogynist — seems like a much safer bet. Why? Because as I've explained, the nuclear family is an inherently patriarchal way of classifying and organizing small groups of kin under a man's control. Even today, it continues to employ the same old gender-based division of labor. Plus, the Oedipal mythology of both murderous ascendancy and daddy–daughter erotic desire are baked right into our predominant understanding of what it takes to be a good dad. Therefore, there's very little reason to think that a family man tacitly cares about women's issues. In some cases he may try, and his conscious intentions may be pure, but there's no escaping the latent misogyny of the nuclear family.

Of course, I'm not suggesting we need to get rid of the nuclear family, although things do seem to be trending in that direction. According to a 2020 Pew report, only three in ten millennials live with a spouse and their own child or children. The majority are not married, or they married much later than previous generations. While forty percent of millennial men between ages twenty-two and thirty-seven have fathered children (compared to forty-six percent of Gen Xers at the same age), only thirty-two percent report living with their biological children (compared with forty-one percent of Gen Xers, forty-four percent of Boomers, and sixty-six percent of the prior generation).[35] Clearly, the nuclear family is less popular than ever. Still, I'm not opposed to it.

I live in a household that approximates the nuclear-family structure. That is, we get as close as we can despite divorce and the limitations of halftime custody. While writing this book, I moved in with my partner, Amanda, and her two children, who, like mine, spend half their time living in our home. We're as close to nuclear as a family of stepsiblings, stepchildren, and stepparents can get. We eat dinner together, we have game nights and movie nights, and sibling squabbles are the norm rather than the exception, but when it comes to being a feminist dad, nothing about "going nuclear" makes things easier; it makes them more challenging. Now, I need to be vigilant about remembering that the organization of our household is inherently patriarchal. I must make constant efforts to overcome the intrinsic inequities, and to engage in a version of fatherhood that's intentionally anti-sexist. To this end, I announce my feminist intentions to the whole family regularly, but it's not really enough. "Feminist dad" is not a costume I can pull off the shelf. It's not a political stance that I can silk-screen onto a T-shirt, or a selfie I can post on Instagram. Instead, I need to make proactive choices that affirm my ongoing commitment to gender equality. To do so, I start in the most obvious place: thinking critically about the distribution of household labor.

Studies consistently demonstrate that even in most marriages with proudly progressive husbands — those who proclaim themselves evolved, feminist men — household labor remains unequally distributed. While men have become much more involved in family care over the past few decades, women are still the default caretakers. Author Darcy Lockman explains that even working mothers "devote twice as much time to family care as men."[36] And dads know it; they can't play dumb. Expectant fathers tell researchers that they anticipate that their wives will shoulder more of the new childcare responsibilities. Six months in, the same dads report that they do even less than they initially predicted. Even in households with older kids and teenagers, the same imbalance remains. Whether they're married or divorced coparents, mothers are far more likely than fathers to take responsibility for envisioning, planning, organizing, managing, and executing the logistics of their children's lives. They coordinate transportation to and from soccer games, gather supplies for school trips, keep kids focused on homework assignments, prepare for birthday parties and sleepovers, make appointments for pediatric checkups, and more. How do children make sense of witnessing these discrepancies? What conclusions do they draw about gender? Clearly, the requisite skills needed to accomplish all of these tasks don't track neatly to typically "feminine" competencies, but kids observe their parents and learn to take the unspoken (and oftentimes spoken) sexist expectations of the patriarchal nuclear family for granted.

Fathers, by the way, tend to spend a lot more time playing with their kids — ball on the front lawn, jovial roughhousing and prosocial teasing, joint media engagement and video games.[37] This seems nice, but it also reinforces narcissistic patriarchal authority. Like the old image of the lazy husband, served dinner and beer in front of the football game, it sends kids the message that the home is maintained by women for the purpose of providing a place for male leisure and relaxation. Worse still, when it comes to the business of family care, even the dads who identify as progressive, evolved, and feminist are inclined to see themselves as helpers and babysitters, not the assertive administrators of everyday parenting tasks. They're happy to offer assistance when Mom asks, but when you add all their contributions up, fathers look a lot more like children — albeit obliging older siblings — than equally responsible coparents.

With this in mind, Amanda and I resisted moving in together for a long time. We were both afraid that we might wake up one day to discover that we had accidentally replicated the inequitable gender patterns of the nuclear family. We've been together, in a committed romantic partnership, for a decade. In an essay I once wrote for *The Good Men Project*, I described it this way: "Every day we try to figure out what two natural born rebels with knee-jerk aversion to restriction and constraint need from a relationship. I belong to nobody. She'd say the same. Our mutual closeness is grounded in a kind of distance that's designed to avoid the you-complete-me cliché. Instead, we share a mutual adoration for the other's independence."[38] To reinforce this sentiment, we chose to live separately, constantly telling friends and acquaintances that we weren't moving in together until all the kids had moved out. We were terrified that passion and affection for each other would be superseded by resentment and frustration.

One day, during the coronavirus pandemic, we changed our minds. We talked about how habitual text messages and weekly face-to-face date nights no longer satisfied our mutual desire for a pervasive sense of partnership. We both wanted someone special with whom to share the daily vicissitudes of our lives, and a relationship conducted primarily through digital communications felt inadequate now that most of our time was spent homebound. At least, that's what we told each other, but it could also be that in an atmosphere so riddled with political, medical, and financial uncertainty, we found a new sense of comfort in the familiar, heteronormative model of family. This wasn't a time that called for more disruption of norms! So we went house hunting and now we're living happily ever after.

Princess fairy tales are usually associated with the pink aisle of the toy store, but the truth is that "happily ever after" serves cisgender men more than it serves those who identify as women. No matter how hard the wedding industry tries to frame marriage as the result of "true love" between coequal "soul mates," there's no denying the misogynist history. Heterosexual cohabitation was once contractual and economic — often just an institution that men used to organize women and children as property.[39] So, what can a feminist dad do? He may want to live in a nuclear family and to embrace a binary father-figure identity, but he also wants to combat the collection of beliefs and structures that some theorists call "hetero-patriarchy."[40] He needs to find small everyday ways to avoid reproducing the supposedly neutral dynamics of "straight" partnership.

One thing Amanda and I do is keep score. Of course, the common taken-for-granted wisdom on relationships is that you should never keep score because "true love" is not a competition, but it's clear that if nobody's doing the accounting, the numbers will always skew toward Dad's benefit. There's just too much messaging setting up inequitable gender expectations for anyone to seriously believe that love and dedication alone will steer heterosexual couples toward a copacetic balance.

A feminist dad knows that in a culture where women and men have both been raised to believe the fallacy that a healthy family combines Oedipal Stage 2.0 with narcissistic patriarchal authority, it takes a lot of intentional conversation — and even more checklists — to make sure household responsibilities and family care are handled equitably.

Vagina Dentata

It's revealing that so many of the things I've written about fathers and their daughters have been at least tangentially related to heterosexual eros. It shows how tightly wrapped the tendrils of locker-room gender essentialism can be. Even while trying to deconstruct taken-for-granted sexist beliefs around fatherhood, it's difficult to escape false ideas about the innate tug of opposite-sex attraction. Whether it's the uncomfortable history of symbolic daddy–daughter eroticism or the false pretense of paternalistic protectionism, our attitudes have been profoundly influenced by the problematic assumption that gender identity develops in accordance with a genital binary.

So often, dads tell me about the steep learning curve they had to overcome while discovering how to best raise their daughters. For example, a common refrain I heard while informally interviewing friends and relatives for this book was that it was difficult getting accustomed to girls' emotions, to their fragile psychological dispositions, to their propensity to internalize criticism. Obviously, these are all familiar stereotypes that have been debunked in hundreds of different ways, but even many of the best fathers I know — who would undoubtedly argue against these sexist ideas when it comes to women in the workplace — seem to believe there might be some truth lingering in these troublesome assumptions when it comes to daughters.

I've already made clear throughout this book that I acknowledge that human reproductive anatomy doesn't abide a binary. It's a spectrum, but that doesn't mean there aren't unique challenges involved in fathering those who identify as girls. It just means that the unique challenges are culturally determined. Sure, we all know parents who love to tell us that they didn't paint the nursery or dress their kids in the conventional colors. No blue. No pink. "And still, there were very clear differences between my son and my daughter." That's what one father told me, while we both encouraged our roughhousing sons to act like rebel Jedi fighting the Imperial Sith Fleet. "He likes trucks and fighting! And I don't know how she became such a princess-loving girly-girl! My wife is not like that."

Many parents gravitate toward this kind of ineffectual anecdotal evidence. I guess it's easier to attribute inequality to anatomy than it is to come to terms with your own culpability. We all love our kids and we all hate struggling to protect them from forces that feel out of our control, but a feminist dad must confront the truth. There is so much scholarly social-science research — not to mention an exhaustive amount of popular nonfiction writing — that demonstrates the way cultural attitudes around gender are reproduced. Sexism is ubiquitous and children internalize it no matter how hard their parents try to shelter them. Peers, toy advertisements, and media have a much stronger influence on kids' attitudes than their parents do.[41] Children see coded messages about gender everywhere — toxic masculinity in cartoons, cheerleaders making duck lips on Instagram, Oedipal drama at the movie theater. Author and sociologist Kyl Myers put it nicely: "There's an obsession with penis equals boy and vulva equals girl, and once that's established, the kids get placed on different social conveyor belts and sent through life."[42] Unless you choose gender-creative parenting, as Myers did — using they, them, their pronouns — most of the interactions your child has with adults and other children are guaranteed to include both subtle and overt messages about gender expectations.

If this is so clearly true, why do so many fathers still buy into sexist stereotypes? Why do they experience their daughters' behavior as something cryptic and unfamiliar? Clearly, some of them just refuse to accept the scientific truth. Like flat-earthers, they simply can't be reasoned with. Those men don't really interest me. Neither do the dads who intentionally ignore the facts because they're deliberately trying to maintain the unjust dominance and privilege that patriarchy affords them. I suspect those men aren't reading this book anyway. The dads who do interest me are the ones who are mostly reasonable, but still seem to stubbornly believe that the vagina has mysterious and otherworldly powers—secrets it won't divulge, riddles that science will never untangle. This attitude reminds me of an archetypal motif called *vagina dentata*.

The term *vagina dentata* refers to the image of a vulva encircled with sharp teeth. The most distinct example comes from a Native American myth,[43] but there are cases from all over the world and throughout historical time periods. There are paintings, etchings, and drawings of almond-shaped ovals (sometimes called a *mandorla*)—pointed on the top and bottom like the overlapping section of a Venn diagram—with jagged, protruding fangs circumscribing the border. In Polynesian-Māori legend, Hine-nui-te-pō is the goddess of the underworld. "Her mouth is that of a barracuda, and in the place where men enter her she has sharp teeth of obsidian and greenstone."[44] Disney based their 2016 animated feature *Moana* on Polynesian folklore, but they left this character out of the story.[45] Some traditions have myths imagining that a serpent hides inside the vagina. Sometimes, it's a crab or piranha. In almost all cases, vagina dentata is associated with the idea that something dangerous lurks within something alluring. Even the slang term "pussy" is said to be associated with this archetype — cats are fuzzy, soft, and warm, but they also have razor-sharp claws and teeth.

Many psychoanalysts say vagina dentata represents a fear of castration. In this regard, feminist critic Camille Paglia considers it a pretty straightforward image. "Metaphorically, every vagina has secret teeth, for the male exits as less than when he entered." She writes, "The basic mechanics of conception require action in the male but nothing more than passive receptivity in the female. Sex as a natural rather than social transaction, therefore, really is a kind of drain of male energy by female fullness. Physical and spiritual castration is the danger every man runs in intercourse with a woman."[46] From Paglia's perspective, the idea of a mysterious and otherworldly vagina is associated with men's agonizing dread of so-called emasculation. Certainly you've met fathers who cling to a persona aligned with the 1950s image of the stoic sitcom dad — father, king, commander, provider, protector, breadwinner. Any alternative characterization bruises their egos. Does this explain the confusion certain fathers experience when it comes to raising daughters? Maybe they unconsciously associate the vagina's power with a threat to their strength. *Teena is manipulative; she might outsmart me!* Perhaps they cling to locker-room gender essentialism because becoming fully feminist dads—going all in on responsive fathering—would require surrendering too many comforts and privileges.

The problem with this interpretation is that it's grounded in narcissistic patriarchal authority. It implies that male privilege is valid. As philosopher Luce Irigaray points out, both "castration anxiety" and "penis envy" represent problematic examples of phallocentric thinking. She links it to Freud, explaining how he speculates that our early experience observing opposite-sex parents forms the basis of adult psychology. Freud imagines the first time a child spots the naked adult: The visible organ (penis) is assumed to be normal and the vulva is seen as something lacking rather than something distinct. Irigaray writes, "THERE NEVER IS (OR WILL BE) A LITTLE GIRL." (Her caps.) Instead, little girls are imagined as little boys without penises. In this theory, they're defined by what's absent. Irigaray continues, "'He' *sees* the disadvantage for which 'he' is *anatomically destined*: 'he' has only a tiny little sex organ, no sex organ at all, really, an almost invisible sex organ. The almost imperceptible clitoris."[47] This is locker-room gender essentialism at its worst. There's nothing subtle about it; the misogynistic messaging is explicit. There are not two separate, opposite, and equal anatomical types—it's not *Men Are from Mars, Women Are from Venus*[48]—there's really only one. The anatomical binary is built on a theoretical foundation that considers "maleness" to be neutral and deems all potential alternatives to be pathological.

From this perspective, it's clear that each time a father

expresses bewilderment about raising daughters, he is also unconsciously reinforcing a sexist narrative of child development. Simultaneously, he's doubling down on male privilege. The Jungian perspective makes this even clearer. With characteristically troublesome gender essentialism, Jungians tend to associate vagina dentata with the devouring mother. They think it has to do with an innate anxiety around losing control—that a symbolically "masculine" ego can be swallowed by the symbolically "feminine" unconscious. In other words, the rational and reasonable "male" part of the psyche is always in danger of being chewed up and digested by the dark, incomprehensible, mysterious, and chaotic "female" part of the psyche. *Sigh!* It's an astoundingly sexist articulation of traditional masculine ideology: so-called femininity threatens male visibility.

Each time a man worries about emasculation, he's reinforcing this misogynist ego fallacy. He's not only bemoaning the loss of undeserved privilege that he enjoys because of the institutionalized decrees of "hetero-patriarchy," but he's also doing a disservice to somebody's daughter. To be a feminist dad, you need to reject familiar scripts of both emasculation and anatomy-based bewilderment. Acknowledge that they serve only to normalize sexist, misogynistic, homophobic, and transphobic delusions.

PART FOUR

HOW TO BE A
FEMINIST DAD

SATURDAY, 6:43 A.M.: It's quiet on the back patio of the new house, even with four kids at home. They're lazy. Still asleep. Probably drooling on their pillows until early afternoon. Maybe they're tired from too much YouTube and video games last night. That's fine with me; let them rest. I relish the tranquil, introspective mornings. Everything seems to get harder once the children are awake.

It's not their fault. I see the pattern clearly. My mood shapes their dispositions. They reflect my affect. Their behavior is problematic because mine is, too. My stress becomes theirs — and they don't understand why. They're not the ones with deadlines looming. They're not trying to make sense of the complicated interpersonal dynamics of grown-up relationships. They're not in a persistent state of alarm, watching a world suddenly so full of uncertainty, and wondering what will be left for the next generation. It's not fair; they shouldn't have to confront my emotional burdens.

Of course, I do my best to compartmentalize my feelings. I know I'm not supposed to bring work home with me; I should keep those old Industrial Age divisions clear. But like the diced carrots, peas, and corn on the segmented tray of a Salisbury steak TV dinner, something always slips over the partitions. It's as if trying to hold my feelings in just pushes them further out. Boundaries are porous; things always leak. It makes me wonder why the stoic-dad persona even exists in the first place. Whom does it serve? Not me; the kids see right through it.[1] They interpret my restraint as passive aggression. The quieter I get, the more they keep their distance. Then I watch them interact with one another exactly the way I've been interacting with them: mostly disassociated and cold, with quick, unexpected, and targeted verbal blows.

They mimic my anger and melancholy, and that makes things more severe. I look at them and see the worst parts of myself—my contemptuousness, my immaturity. I'm forty-three years old and I still don't think of myself as a grown-up. Fatherhood was supposed to be a threshold, carrying me toward a palpable sense of adultness. It didn't happen. The ordinary father-figure identity never seemed to fit. Inadequacy became hostility, amplified by self-loathing, and directed outward. It's bad for the kids' psychological well-being, but what am I supposed to do? I'm human; I have feelings. I can't control them, even if I'd like to. There's no way to be perfect for my kids every time they need it. They need it all the time, not only to cook meals and drive them to and from school, but also to be a model of stability and fulfillment. Being a dad is not a job with coffee breaks and lunch hours. It's exhausting.

Sometimes I try being transparent. Driving with my fifteen-year-old in the passenger seat, I turn off the radio and let it all out. *I'm sorry I seem angry, it's not you, I'm just aggravated because nothing feels easy, everything is so complicated, there's pressure from your mother and your stepmom, and my book is due, plus I wrote a great essay and all the op-ed sections keep rejecting it, I don't have time for a rewrite because there are so many students, and the students are frustrated that COVID-19 has pushed classes online, so I want to be there for them, build rapport, give them the kind of acknowledgment that usually requires just a smile or remembering to follow up on something personal they said in class, but now it's at least fifteen minutes of Zoom office hours for each one of them, and I don't have time to do it the way I wish I could because I also have to cook dinner and order the groceries, and mop the floor, and help you with your homework.* He looks at me, unsure how to respond. Confused. Overwhelmed. Speechless.

I stop at a red light and put my hand on his shoulder. *You don't have to say anything. It's not your problem, but thanks for listening.* He seems relieved, but I instantly regret the whole episode. It's not that I wish I hadn't revealed vulnerability; it's not that I'm afraid of appearing weak, like I don't have everything under control. Instead, it's because I don't know if he's really equipped to make sense of all the things I just said. What if he internalizes it? What if he thinks some of it is his fault? When I'm at my lowest, I don't have the wherewithal to contextualize my emotions for him. I don't have the presence of mind to speak with intention. Besides, it's not his job to be my sounding board. He's not supposed to be my anchored confidant. It's not okay for me to put him in that position.

The experts would tell me to revisit it another time — sit down and have a thoughtful conversation with him when the tension is not so high. Later I'll be happy, he'll be relieved that I'm happy, and he won't want to engage in a serious conversation. He'll want to ride the euphoria. He'll want to joke around and act silly. We'll sit on the sofa, he'll nod, pretending to listen. His mind will be elsewhere — probably on some video game. When I tell him he can go play, he'll trot up the stairs, goofy with joy. I'll stay alone for a few more moments, wondering if he'd sometimes prefer a different kind of dad. He sees the hero's journey on display in just about every story he watches on Netflix and Amazon Prime. Maybe he already believes the Oedipal lies. Maybe he thinks a boy needs his father to model the real world's apathy and indifference. Maybe he doesn't want a feminist dad.

Sometimes my younger son asks me why I can't "just be normal, like all the other dads." He tells me I overthink things. He teases me, saying that one day he'll have to go to psychotherapy to talk about how I always pressured him to be divergent. He'll cry to his shrink about the trauma and anxiety associated with not being allowed to conform to ordinary, familiar measures of academic or social success. *My dad was nuts! I'd ask him to help with my math homework and he'd start ranting and raving about "implicit gender bias" in the word problems.* True story.

Do my kids get what I'm doing? Why I'm doing it? Do they understand that I'm fathering in a way that aims to disrupt the status quo? Everyone prefers what's easily recognizable, but I refuse to parent in ways that prepare children to reap the familiar dividends of rugged individualism. That model of autonomy is sexist, misogynist, and outdated. The imperialist, capitalist, white supremacist, hetero-patriarchal norms need to be challenged. Of course, that doesn't mean that every straight, white American dad who's trying to accumulate wealth is a villain. You can be all those things. It's fine, provided you don't pathologize and disenfranchise everything other.

It all comes down to what we consider to be "normal." And a feminist dad knows that there is no normal.

Critical Consciousness

The first principle of becoming a feminist dad is to cultivate *critical consciousness*. The term "critical consciousness" comes from the iconic Brazilian educator Paulo Freire. He also called it "conscientization." It describes the skill set — or maybe I should call it a mindset — that enables a person to reflect, analyze, interpret, and then revise their personal account of lived experience. You might think it sounds easy, but it's not.

To understand why, consider the myriad social, cultural,

economic, and political structures that constitute the context within which we all go about our daily lives. The jobs we perform, the technologies we operate, the communities in which we worship, and the media we view all play a part in determining the categories we use to evaluate our experience of reality. This is what people mean when they say that gender is culturally constructed. Narratives and images are all around us. They establish expectations and shape our preferences for taking on certain roles. They also influence our decisions about which personas we want to adopt. Familiar stories urge us toward predictable patterns, contouring our habits and molding our routines. External pressures also form the frameworks through which we understand internal psychological phenomena, creating the consummate prototypes—the ideals and exemplars—against which we measure ourselves. Often we don't even realize the degree to which our identity narratives are influenced by outside forces. It feels as if our dreams and aspirations arose from within; therefore, we fail to recognize that the attitudes we've elected to adopt are also conventions to which we've conformed. We accept the aggregate experience of our lives without contemplating the origins of its constituent parts.

Like the fish in David Foster Wallace's famous 2005 Kenyon College commencement speech, we have to keep reminding ourselves: This is water.[2] That's because it's never easy to see the reality in which you're swimming. Everyday systems, stories, and customs ebb and flow like the tide. They blend into an all-encompassing current that you barely recognize most of the time. You're sometimes shocked to find yourself engaged in behaviors — or habits of mind — that betray your values. It's almost involuntary. You wanted to paddle upstream, and maybe you tried; but when you take a breath, you discover that you're still floating along with the current. Likewise, you may want nothing more than to become a feminist dad, but you continue to inadvertently reinforce the same old patriarchal narratives. It's almost impossible for you to stop. Why? Because you can't really self-reflect. It feels too painful to acknowledge your own limitations.

It's not that you can't admit when you're wrong. In most cases, you probably can. You may even embrace discomfort — after all, the contemporary self-help, spirituality, and personal development movements are almost masochistic in their definitions of what constitutes adequate transformative catharsis. Primal screams and evacuant tears are par for the course. There is status and prestige in the kind of emotional self-flagellation that psycho-spiritual retreats and boot camps depend on, but even those who subscribe to these therapeutic models struggle when it comes to acknowledging how troublesome their commitment to locker-room gender essentialism can be. Evasion feels like the only safe bet. It's a defense mechanism — necessary because on some level, we all recognize that owning up to our fallacies and failures would involve serious demolition work. We'd have to deconstruct a lifetime's worth of virtues, choices, and ideas.

Everything crumbles when a person's ideological foundation loses its structural integrity, so I wouldn't blame you for dodging the tough questions. In Joseph Campbell's monomyth this resistance is called "Refusal of the Call." He wrote, "The refusal is essentially a refusal to give up what one takes to be one's best interest."[3] He says at first all heroes avoid looking at their contextual problems, because forestalling a quest provides us with the Don Quixote delusion that we're in control of our own narratives, but it never really works because we also know that any sense of satisfaction we might get from the egocentric act of denial will ultimately be short-lived. That's why today's fathers are struggling. A nagging voice incessantly reminds us that our avoidance of feminism is galvanized not by agency or autonomy, but rather by a fear of losing the familiar comforts of male privilege.

So, what's the alternative? How can we truly take control of our actions? How can we become proactive about changing the way we imagine ourselves as father figures? How can we transform the ways we respond to the world? For that, we need to cultivate critical consciousness, and to understand what this entails, it's helpful to consider Paulo Freire's work in detail.

Freire is famous for his progressive education theory. You may have heard people complain about "the banking model of education" — in which lecturers stand at the front of a room and *deposit* academic content into their students' empty minds. That metaphor is borrowed from Paulo Freire.[4] Maybe you've been to a back-to-school night during which enthusiastic teachers or school administrators talked about replacing the "sage on the stage" with a "guide on the side." They tell you how your kids will take an active role in their own learning this year, how your children will follow their unique interests, become passionate scholars, develop study projects independently and in small groups. These are educational possibilities that wouldn't be nearly as common and widely accepted had it not been for the subversive work of Paulo Freire.

Freire believed that when we see learning as the transmission of wisdom and knowledge from one extraordinary expert to a group of imperfect and incomplete students, we're limiting human potential and hindering educational outcomes. Why? Because we're reinforcing the idea that systemic inequality is part of the ordinary, natural, and normal order of things. The traditional vertical hierarchy of school sends covert, coded messages about power and agency. Students learn to see the world through the framework they've witnessed and participated in, and the relationship between authority and subjugate becomes second nature. Therefore, in all their future endeavors, students will tend toward one familiar role or the other — leader or follower, oppressor or oppressed, dominant or submissive. From this perspective, every teacher should be asking: How is the classroom engineered? What subtle messages does the design communicate? What assumptions are embedded in our everyday learning processes? Which students are presumed to be in need of paternalistic assistance? And who's considered self-sufficient?

Every father figure should apply the same thinking to the practice of child-rearing. He should ask: How is our family organized? What messages do our everyday habits, routines, and relations communicate to our children? What are they learning about authority, exploitation, service, and compla-cency? What does my approach to intervention and discipline say to children about justice and retribution? Whom do they see taking responsibility for which household chores? Who gives advice to whom? How does the family arrive at the big life decisions that affect us all? Questions like these are at the root of critical consciousness.

Freire called instructors "animators" rather than "teachers." Their job is not to present ideas, deliver content, or manage classroom behaviors. It's to spark curiosity, animate critical consciousness, and inspire conversation. The way you frame your responsibilities — the way you see yourself in relationship to your duties — changes the way you approach the work. Don't fall into the trap of replicating "oppressor consciousness," which Freire says has a sadistic tendency to "'in-animate' everything and everyone it encounters."[5] In the same way, a father should always be considering the ways in which his par-ticipation in the dynamics of the family animate or in-animate its members. Bottom line: a feminist dad can't see himself as the dominant head of the hetero-patriarchal household unless he wants to acclimate his children to troublesome ideas about gender, authority, and power.

To emphasize this point, there's one more thing you should know about Paulo Freire. He originally worked with under-privileged adults, teaching literacy skills, but his pedagogy was always about more than just the mechanics and techniques of reading and writing. He wrote, "Acquiring literacy does not involve memorizing sentences, words, or syllables — lifeless objects unconnected to an existential universe — but rather an attitude of creation and recreation, a self-transformation producing a stance of intervention in one's context."[6] What he means is that the purpose of education, no matter the topic, should be to liberate the autonomous human subject, to enable a person to play an active role in claiming the right to shape their own reality. Freire saw how often people feel helpless — disempowered by propaganda-like narratives that suggest that things are beyond their control. He recognized that so many folks mistakenly believe they can't intervene and manipulate the context of their own existence. In truth, they just don't have the language to do so. They feel like objects rather than subjects. They're adapted, rather than integrated, into their context. That's why "critical consciousness" is so important. It involves learning to "read" the way oppressive power structures function; and it's about providing people with the tools necessary to transform their world, to "author" their own stories. Psychologists Mary Watkins and Helene Shulman summarize it nicely: "Critical consciousness involves decoding the social lies that naturalize the status quo, while searching for alternative interpretations of one's situation."[7]

How does this apply to fathers? For a feminist dad, fatherhood requires adopting routines and habits that intentionally develop your children's capacity for critical consciousness. This means you prioritize their intellectual authority, their ability to arrive at their own conclusions. Show your children that you admire it when they construct unique ideas and opinions. One way to do this is by asking tough questions for which you don't already have correct answers in mind. That's the important part: Don't bother asking if you already know the response you'd prefer to hear. You don't want to be judging whether their thoughts are aligned with yours. Instead, you want to engage with their alternative perspectives, show them that you value their process and their voice.

Many parents try to demonstrate this kind of respect for their children with excessive praise. *Great idea. You're so smart. I love what you just said.* Grown-ups mistakenly imagine that constant veneration helps to build confidence, but from a feminist dad's perspective, this strategy is only slightly better than toxic tough love. Sure, positive language is preferable to negative; compliments are better than criticisms, but superficial flattery still sets up a transactional hierarchy of rewards, teaching young people to equate self-worth with approval from authority figures. It becomes their habit to seek endorsement from those with higher social status. Therefore, feigned admiration does very little to encourage critical consciousness. Instead, you need to show respect through your actions. Demonstrate a willingness to engage with them as intellectual subjects. Have real debates with your children, push them to support their arguments, challenge their positions the same way you would a colleague's. Show that you take them seriously by treating them with dignity, rather than paternalism.

My son loves to have "smart arguments" at the dinner table. He never wants them to stop. We'll debate totally inane things—the ethics of Elon Musk; what counts as a tower defense game; are natural phenomena *caused* by "science," or is science just a descriptive language? Sometimes it's all seman-tics and it gets tiresome. It devolves into rhetorical nonsense, but because my overarching goal is to train him to take a stance of intervention, to feel empowered to shape his own reality, I don't want to shut it down. I do my best to avoid playing the role of intellectual authority. I don't want to be a father figure who decrees the final truth. Oftentimes it's difficult for me to conjure the necessary humility to stop the debate in a construc-tive way. I frequently fail. I make the mistake of saying, "I'm bored," or, "I'm done with this conversation." That's no good—it tells him that Dad's whims should determine how things conclude. Alternatively, on my good days, I say, "I think we've reached a standstill, so let's both do more research on this sub-ject and then revisit this discussion another night." We never revisit it, because neither of us actually cared about the content. It was all about the process.

Cultivating your children's critical consciousness is super important, but it's not enough for feminist dads. We have an even more significant duty to cultivate our own critical consciousness—and that should raise some eyebrows. Why? Because Freire worked with disenfranchised populations, teach-ing oppressed people that they have more agency and autonomy than they recognize. But clearly, under patriarchy, dads are not disenfranchised. If anything, we're the oppressors, not the oppressed. The privileges of narcissistic patriarchal authority are ours for the taking, so does it really make any sense to apply Freire's model to the very people most likely to benefit from an imperialist, white supremacist, capitalist hetero-patriarchy? I think so, because despite their exalted social status, fathers are not really free. Like everyone else, we're also confined by sexist ideologies. We're saddled with expectations that define what it means to feel like a father and act like a man. We're told it's a man's world, but our choices for how to live in it are severely limited.

Please don't misunderstand me. Don't jump to the conclusion that I'm describing the same old familiar burdens of toxic masculinity. I'm not. The truth is I find a lot of the contemporary rhetoric claiming cisgender men need more opportunities to express vulnerable emotions to be severely oversimplified. To put it crudely, it often sounds to me like a bunch of boys whining, "Somebody please, hold my balls while I cry!" Let's be honest: if you already have unwarranted access to everything — including the authority to construct your own narrative — do you really need explicit permission to go to therapy, too? Isn't that just claiming yet another privilege? Isn't that the definition of entitlement? Yes and no.

The view that men need more opportunities to engage in affective experiences that have long been associated with femininity is reductive and problematic. It assumes that holistic well-being comes from a union of so-called feminine and so-called masculine traits. Therefore it recapitulates the same old gender essentialism that primarily serves to maintain the patriarchal status quo. With critical consciousness, there's a more refined way to understand the constrictive pressures of manhood, as well as the constrictive pressures of fatherhood. As bell hooks explains, "Patriarchy as a system has denied males access to full emotional well-being, which is not the same as feeling rewarded, successful, and powerful because of one's capacity to assert control over others."[8] She's pointing out that men don't experience patriarchal power the way pop feminism typically imagines they do. It's not simply the inverse of the suppression and disrespect that women suffer as the result of institutionalized misogyny. Men don't feel like they're reaping the rewards of dominance. There's no victory party happening in their heads. Instead, most men feel humiliated and frustrated by their lack of access to the power that patriarchy claims to bestow.

Of course, it's unconscious. Men can't own up to it because they've been taught never to acknowledge feelings of diminishment or degradation. These are not considered "manly" emotions. To its credit, the discourse on toxic masculinity gets this part right. The problem is that, in most cases, the social pressure to repress vulnerability is framed as an affront to men's liberated individual autonomy. What's seen as "unjust" is men's lack of access to true, unencumbered narcissistic patriarchal authority. *Why can't my story include disappointment, melancholy, helplessness? It's not fair that all my feelings can't be acknowledged and expressed.* If this is how you see the problem, then the obvious solution — more opportunities for cathartic release — is inherently ineffectual. It does nothing to identify or disrupt the sexist, misogynistic, homophobic, and transphobic status quo that created the problem in the first place. Therefore, in the long run, it's bound to reproduce more of the same toxic experiences for everyone.

To be a feminist dad, try to look at the same situation with the bird's-eye view that characterizes critical consciousness. See how you can take responsibility and acknowledge culpability. Recognize that you already have the agency required to transform your reality. You just need the vocabulary necessary to address the real problem. You know it's undeniable that men, as a group, are elevated to a position of social dominance, but as individuals we're losing the homosocial battle for so-called alpha-male status more often than we're winning it. According to sociologist Michael Kimmel, "We've constructed the rules of manhood so that only the tiniest fraction of men come to believe that they are the biggest of wheels, the sturdiest of oaks, the most virulent repudiators of femininity, the most daring and aggressive."[9] Hence, we mansplain when we can, because we feel like most of the time, we can't. Therefore, cisgender men don't necessarily need more opportunities to talk about our feelings, to feel redeemed, to validate our own Don Quixote delusions. But we do need help learning how to resolve the tension between the promised exultation of father-figure identity and the inevitable feelings of inadequacy that accompany the patriarchal, winner-takes-all competition to dominate others. We need to find distance from our triggered emotions so that we can imagine new, more equitable, and more fulfilling ways to navigate our relationships.

To be a feminist dad, look at the processes of acculturation and socialization from the meta-perspective that critical consciousness allows. See how the privileges of patriarchy harm men as well as everyone else. Recognize that all the implicit signifiers of manhood are designed to misdirect our attention, and to fortify the status quo. Therefore, instead of looking at our own behaviors—and accepting accountability for the way we reinforce problematic patterns—we often scapegoat anyone or anything that urges us to examine the ideological tyranny of what-goes-without-saying.[10] We blame feminists, LGBTQ+ activists, elite liberal college professors, cancel-culture tweeps, and the supposed devaluation of the masculine ideal.[11] We refuse the call.

To be a feminist dad, you need to answer the call. That's why so much of this book has been about uncovering everyday routines and assumptions that reinforce the structures of patriarchy. The reflexive process of social and cultural analysis is itself a feminist action. It's urgent that dads take responsibility for identifying the ordinary elements of fatherhood that model sexism, exploitation, and oppression. It's also time we become attuned to the misogynistic, homophobic, and transphobic symbolism of patriarchy. Stop complaining when people call it out; start calling it out yourself. For far too long, we've been complacent in our self-serving cultural illiteracy.

Responsive Fathering

The second principle of becoming a feminist dad is to practice *responsive fathering*. At first glance, the concept seems so simple and obvious that it barely needs an explanation. Just listen and respond more to your children, partners, and spouses. Dictate and command less. Sounds easy enough, but putting it into practice is trickier than you think.

Many fathers believe they're being receptive and amenable, but self-interest and egocentricity still shape their dispositions and demeanors. It happens in surreptitious ways because no matter how hard dads try to put other people first, they can't shake the cultural assumption that a father figure is the sovereign progenitor — the wisest, smartest, most creative person, leading every conversation. That's why, throughout this book, I've framed responsive fathering in contrast to *narcissistic patriarchal authority*. I wanted to interrogate the way dads are taught to imagine their own voices — louder and more significant than the rest of the family's. I wanted to show some of the ways fathers unconsciously reproduce the expectation that they marshal the rest of humankind through an inherently patriarchal history.

These days, we hear a lot about mansplaining and interrupting. While it makes sense to frame the inclination toward officiousness as an offense, reproach alone doesn't help men recognize how their bad behaviors fit into a larger picture of systemic inequality. Ultimately, wagging a finger and rebuking them isn't a very effective strategy. Either it makes men feel like scolded children — defensive and obstinate — or it turns the problematic conduct into an easy target for simplistic behavioral modification. The latter is certainly better than the former, but in neither case have men been equipped with adequate tools for considering how mansplaining and interrupting fit into the larger, more troublesome narrative of patriarchal manhood. It's a perfect example of addressing the symptom instead of the cause.

What men really need is help understanding how an authoritative inclination to dominate the story fits into the broader context of father-figure identity. That's why I considered myths, fairy tales, *Star Trek*, and Steve Jobs in part two. I wanted to demonstrate that narcissistic patriarchal authority is nestled at the core of our collective understanding about what it means to be a successful, autonomous person. Gaslighting and Don Quixote delusions are mixed up in our beliefs about selfhood, fulfillment, individualism, and satisfaction. Our theoretical conception of psychological maturity is intricately enmeshed with the fallacies of fatherhood.

When it comes to mansplaining and gaslighting, we recognize that patriarchal narcissistic authority is problematic, but consider that there are many instances in which we appreciate Dad's ability to "make it so." Students in my university classroom regularly write papers about important lessons they've learned from their fathers — and they're always responding to philosophical prompts unrelated to family. Think of how often you hear platitudes that begin with "as my father always says..." The cliché is to reminisce fondly about the times when Dad taught us to repair a flat tire, toss a football, ride a bike, or fix a leaky faucet — then draw an analogy and turn it into an inspirational life lesson. This is the seemingly rosy side of narcissistic patriarchal authority: well-meaning paternal advice. *Father knows best!* Of course, sometimes it is great to learn from a wise elder who has the benefit of practical experience, but this image of the father figure is complicated because the line between patriarch atop his throne, authorizing the truth, and a more democratic Sherpa guide, who simply helps to clear a tangled path, is blurry and ambiguous. Good intentions can become "father always gets the final say" very quickly.

This is where critical consciousness meets responsive fathering. A feminist dad needs to take a bird's-eye view and be aware of the difference between dominating a narrative and listening to what materializes from the cacophony of colliding myths. He needs to ask hard questions such as: How can I participate in my loved ones' lives without dominating? How can I be part of an emergent process of maturation and development without claiming apex status? What does it look like for a father to share what he knows, without knowing best? The answer to all of these questions is responsive fathering. Obviously, it's about trying to be heard less and listen more, but listening is not as simple as it sounds.

Contemporary French philosopher Jean-Luc Nancy distinguishes between "listening" (*l'écoute*) and "understanding" (*l'entente*). In French, both terms have to do with hearing, and Nancy is playing poetic language games to make a philosophical point about what's involved in the act of listening. He points out that "to be all ears" involves a "tension and a balance," a negotiation "between a sense (that one listens to) and a truth (that one understands)."[12] His overall argument is complex, and most of the details aren't relevant to responsive fathering, but it's worth borrowing the basic distinction. It's a framework that feminist dads can use to help them evaluate whether they're parenting with paternalistic authority or humanistic responsibility. Simply put, listening is about hearing; it has to do with receiving a sensation, with reception. In contrast, understanding is a process of thinking — it requires intention. It involves interpretation and analysis. A feminist dad needs to lean toward listening, and yet, all our father-figure inclinations urge us toward understanding.

Consider how, in so many of our interactions with our families, we take on the role of the problem solver. We become fix-it-up handymen, ready to strap on our tool belts and repair anything that's broken — both literally and metaphorically. One mega-popular YouTube channel offers "practical 'Dadvice' for everyday tasks." The creator, Rob Kenney, calls his subscribers — almost 3 million of them at the time of this writing — "my kids." He teaches them how to grill, how to change engine oil, how to start a campfire, and more. In one of the most popular episodes, he tells the audience, "I love you, I'm proud of you, God bless you." But even that was framed as problem-solving. As he told NPR, "A lot of people have never heard their parents say that to them."[13] He's always fixing things.

We might call this version of the father figure "Bricoleur Dad."[14] The word *bricoleur* describes a jack-of-all-trades, somebody who can figure out how to fix anything. In French, the term is associated with tinkering. In French-Canadian primary schools, "faire du bricolage" means doing arts and crafts. The Old French verb *bricole* means going back and forth.

Understand the etymology in two different ways. First, it has to do with moving to and fro, rapidly accomplishing many small chores. Second, it has to do with drawing from a variety of miscellaneous sources and assembling them into something new and useful. It's similar to what folks mean when they use *MacGyver* as a verb, referencing the popular television series from the 1980s and '90s, and referring to improvising makeshift solutions. We become Bricoleur Dad not only when we take a bunch of random materials from the garage and somehow get the garbage disposal working again, but also when we weave random life stories and dad jokes into paternalistic advice. Bricoleur Dad thinks he's being adaptable and extemporaneous, but he's actually bending the situation toward his tool set. He thinks he's listening, but it's more like understanding. It's another attempt to sort other people's experiences into categories that fit Dad's narrative reality.

When I was a kid, my father had hundreds of little baby-food jars lined up on a shelf in the basement. Each one was full of loose screws, nuts, bolts, nails, tacks — organized by shape and size. He could always find exactly what he needed, exactly when he needed it. I don't think I could ever be so organized; my workspace is always a jumble of half-read books, hand-scribbled notes, and way more USB cords than one person needs. I can barely begin to imagine how my father ever found the time to sort through all that hardware. In my rarely used toolbox, all the odds and ends are mixed together on the bottom. I rifle through with my bare hands and my fingertips end up scraped and scratched by the time I find what I'm after. My pride is wounded even more than my hands. I feel like a failure — like I'm not really a grown-up yet. No salve will fix that.

I can't help but associate my dad's methodical tidiness with maturity. That's not just because he's my personal role model. Sorting and partitioning have been historically associated with fatherhood. It fits with the hospital cord-cutting ritual and the Oedipal disruption of the mother–infant bond. The father figure is often seen as a symbolic divider — sectioning the world like a Salisbury steak TV dinner. In fact, before he became hurler of lightning bolts, Zeus dethroned his father, Kronos, King of Titans, whose name literally means "to cut." So it's unsurprising that dads sometimes compartmentalize things even when it's unnecessary. It's a useful thing when it comes to sorting a whole mess of loose screws, nuts, bolts, nails, and tacks, but there can also be a dark side. Think about gender binaries, nationalist categories, and overly partisan politics.

When the patriarchal inclination to sort is too strong, it becomes an ego fallacy. That means you think of it as an innate characteristic of masculinity or fatherhood, and then it can quickly become the kind of partisan or sectarian separation that leads to sexism, homophobia, transphobia, and other prejudices. "Sectarianism is predominantly emotional and uncritical. It is arrogant, antidialogical and thus anticommunicative. It is a reactionary stance," writes Paulo Freire. "The Sectarian creates nothing because he cannot love. Disrespecting the choices of others, he tries to impose his own choice on everyone else."[15] It's almost as if Freire wrote these words to help us see how the well-meaning Bricoleur Dad fails to be responsive.

When you approach everything from the fix-it-up, handyman perspective of problem-solving, you're inclined to deny others an opportunity to be sensed in their own way. You're too busy trying to fit them into your categories. You're in-animating everything and everyone because you're asking them to abide the framing that best serves the father. The alternative is responsive fathering. I love the word *responsive* because it reminds me of an old technological term. Web developers sometimes talk about "responsive web design." Put simply, it means designing a site so that it adapts to the user's display. It may seem obvious to you, but when smartphones were new, most websites didn't take the visitor's platform, screen size, and orientation into account. Responsive Design was about building websites that were attentive to the specific limitations of any given device. It's the reason why, if you log in to my website from your phone, you're going to get a page that's different from what you'd get if you logged in from your laptop or desktop browser. The site responds to the context in which it will be viewed.

Responsive fathering works the same way. You recognize that each engagement with a child (or a partner/spouse) involves unique and individual processes of contextualization. Like a site on different devices, reality renders in different ways for different people. Okay, that's obvious. We all know that everyone has their own perspective, their own way of classifying and categorizing, but consider that narcissistic patriarchal authority expects others to adjust their vision to correspond with Dad's frame.

To practice responsive fathering, you need to adjust your own narrative to meet the frame of your family. You need to receive others without trying to understand how they sort into your baby-food jars.

Anti–Gender Essentialism

The third principle of becoming a feminist dad is to commit to raising your children in an environment devoid of *locker-room gender essentialism.* I can think of only one time that I used the phrase "that's what it means to be a man" with my kids. It was after dinner. I was annoyed that they ran off to play video games before the kitchen was clean, so I sat them both down and said, "From now on, I expect that anytime somebody cooks you dinner — whether it's me, your mom, your grandparents, or a friend's parent — before you leave the kitchen, you'll ask if there's anything else you can do to help clean up. I know you don't want to, but that's basic etiquette. And that's what it means to be a man." I didn't really intend it in terms of gender; I meant it in terms of maturity. Still, I misspoke. I should've said, "That's what it means to be an adult."

In our household, I do most of the cooking. It makes me happy. I also like that the kids witness a different gendered organization of domestic labor from what they regularly see on TV and at the movies, but the real reason I do it has nothing to do with that. Instead, it's just because I'm a better cook than Amanda. Plus, after years of owning and operating professional restaurants, I have terrible dictatorial habits and expectations when it comes to food preparation. I don't like it when people are in my workspace. I hate when they put things away in the wrong cabinet. It aggravates me when the ingredients in the refrigerator aren't labeled and rotated. It drives me nuts when the countertops and other equipment aren't cleaned and sanitized in accordance with health code. That's why there's a chair in *my* kitchen — right across from the commercial, stainless-steel worktable — where Amanda usually sits and keeps me company while I make dinner. I don't want her help. It's much easier for me to produce lots of food for a bunch of hungry tweens and teens alone.

In this instance, our challenge to gender essentialism is unrelated to cultural presumptions about who belongs in the kitchen. We're not being contrarian. We're not trying to do the opposite of what's typically expected. There's a much more nuanced approach to gender equality at play. We try to divide household chores and parenting duties based solely on what fits well into our specific family dynamic. We distribute responsibilities according to each other's skill sets and preferences. Before we moved in together, we stood in front of a big white dry-erase board and mapped out a plan. We were concerned that if we allowed our roles to emerge extemporaneously, without setting clear intentions first, the old gender conventions would creep in and influence us in clandestine ways. We didn't want to unconsciously assume that the other person would do certain jobs without thinking about where those expectations come from.

Honestly, we abandoned the original plan pretty quickly after moving day. Neither of us is organized enough to keep to a regular cleaning or housework schedule. Still, that initial conversation made a huge difference—it revealed a lot of assumptions and I suspect it also prevented a lot of arguments. Now that we're improvising, we use the dry-erase board to keep score; accounting prevents us from inadvertently reproducing notions of "neutral" that are inherently sexist. This approach to chores is partially about maintaining the goodwill, equality, respect—and therefore also the passion—in our relationship. More important, we worry that anytime we abide by old norms, our children will end up believing that what they witnessed in our home should be reproduced in their future relationships.

Recently, we realized that the kids think I'm the boss—that I set the household rules and Amanda obediently follows behind. Clearly, this is out of alignment with my intentions to be a feminist dad; the kids are perceiving exactly the kind of stereotypical power dynamic that we're trying so hard to challenge, so we sat them down and had a long conversation about it. Are they making gendered assumptions? Is it because of power dynamics they've observed in other people's homes? Is it that my more assertive and opinionated style feels authoritative to them? Are they witnessing patterns between the adults that have been established because of convenience and then jumping to the conclusion that it's nonconsensual? Certainly, I often play the bad cop when necessary, but it almost always follows a conversation Amanda and I have had about intentional child-rearing.

The kids all sat on the sofa and we passed a "talking stick" around while asking questions and sharing observations. Ultimately, we didn't really care why the children believed I was in charge — we could never be sure anyway; kids their ages aren't developmentally capable of articulating sophisticated interpretations of their own biases. Rather, it was the discussion that mattered to us. Of course, the kids hate family meetings, but we wanted to model a process of consistently interrogating household roles. It's important for kids to see that nothing about the jobs their parents do should be taken for granted. Our patterns and choices are not fixed and immutable. They're dynamic and fluid. A feminist dad uses conversations like these not only to demonstrate a commitment to anti–gender essentialism, but also to cultivate his children's critical consciousness.

Of course, gender essentialism gets modeled for kids through more than just tedious family meetings and the distribution of chores. There are so many small, seemingly superficial interactions among parents, children, and siblings that can reproduce problematic ideas. One that I'm especially troubled by is "bro-ism" between father and son. *Bro-ism* is a term I use to refer to the way men and boys often talk in coded language, as well as the way they use gestural and behavioral mannerisms.[16] It masquerades as the acceptable and preferred social etiquette of male community building. It's usually boastful and vulgar, implicitly demeaning to women, and brazenly homo- and transphobic. Just think back to your own middle school locker room and you'll remember hundreds of examples. *That's what she said! You're gay! You throw like a girl! Don't be a pussy! Douche!* Bro-ism's messages are delivered as though they're playful and inoffensive. For many dads, a tempered form of bro-ism seems like a reasonable way to encourage father–son bonding. *That waitress would be pretty if she'd smile more. Those were some good-looking girls I saw you talking to after school; way to go, dude!* It's unfortunate that so many father figures inadvertently reinforce bro-ism at home — commenting about "hot" newscasters and winking while making jokes about women's emotional instability or intellectual inferiority. Worse still, some of the combative and sexually violent metaphors men often use unapologetically while talking to their children about sports are so insensitive and disgusting that I won't put them in print. To be a feminist dad, you need to acknowledge that this is one way young men become initiated into the "brotherhood" of male entitlement. Recognize that bro-ism is just an expression of narcissistic patriarchal authority that's been encrypted to seem innocuous.

I hated bro-ism when I was a kid. I couldn't identify it then, but I always knew something felt off about the typical etiquette of male camaraderie. I learned to participate, since my social standing in the middle school boys' locker room depended on it, but it always confused me, especially when it came from adults. Every positive message I got about the ethics of mature manhood was contradicted by witnessing the negative every-day conduct of bro-ism. I was encouraged to look up to kind, compassionate men who also committed rhetorical violence.

The words and phrases they sometimes used betrayed their mostly benevolent dispositions. That left me puzzled, desperately trying to understand how the affirmative messages I received about equality and dignity could be untangled from the misogynist messages that I simultaneously received about belonging and status.

Kids should not have to reconcile the tensions of blatantly contradictory aspirational ideologies. Parents should do it for them. That's why feminist dads need to make a commitment to disrupting bro-ism. There's nothing okay about it; it's never "just a joke." So-called guy talk sends a message to young people about conditions under which misogynist, homophobic, and transphobic speech becomes acceptable (there are none). Worse still, when dads engage in bro-ism with their kids, they reinforce the validity of locker-room gender essentialism. To be a feminist dad, call bro-ism out when you see it or hear it, whether it comes from adults or children. Don't be afraid to correct yourself — in front of your kids — when you inevitably fall into prior patterns. Most of us have been socially conditioned to engage in bro-ism, so the habit is hard to kick. Keep trying and don't get discouraged.

Note that I'm not simply calling bro-ism toxic masculinity. Nor am I advocating softer, noncompetitive, less aggressive, or so-called feminine ways of being. It is critically important for feminist dads to remember that combating gender essentialism is not tantamount to psychological gender bending. It's not about acting "more feminine" or "less masculine." Any framing that depends on attributing affective or cognitive characteristics according to the old false binary continues to reinforce the gender essentialist foundation of patriarchal misogyny — as well as homophobia and transphobia. Simply put, it's more of that "baby-food jar" thinking. The propensity to assemble your view of human characteristics according to the binary logic of "masculine" and "feminine" types is sectarian, narcissistic, and authoritarian. You're not trying to make sense of the people around you responsively; you're expecting the people around you to conform to a way of sorting and categorizing that imposes disenfranchising notions of "normal."

A feminist dad knows that each and every way of organizing individuals has an embedded logic, a configuration that prevents some people from being free. When we think gender ambiguity can be a solution to bro-ism we're relying on a naïve narrative of pseudo-equality. It says things are separate but equal, but the things that don't fit into your existing baby-food jars are not, in your mind, equal to those that do. They're marginalized and excluded. Outsiders. Therefore, all forms of locker-room gender essentialism are inherently coercive and constrictive. They limit our beliefs about what's possible and pathologize anything disenfranchised by heteronormative, white supremacist, capitalist patriarchy.

Commit to raising your children in an environment devoid of locker-room gender essentialism. Establish familial roles according to skill sets and preferences, not cultural norms. Show your kids that you're committed to constantly questioning taken-for-granted assumptions about who should do certain jobs and accomplish specific tasks. Avoid bonding with children through "guy talk" and "girl's night" because most conventional notions of gendered camaraderie reinforce sexist expectations, conceal the mechanics of systemic misogyny, and maintain the exclusionary patterns of patriarchal dominance.

Rigorous Inclusivity

The fourth principle of becoming a feminist dad is to be *rigorously inclusive*. It requires extending your commitment to respect, dignity, and equality beyond issues of gender. It involves applying critical consciousness indiscriminately: interrogating all instances of systematized oppression and recognizing the ways in which signs, symbols, patterns, and narratives normalize unjust social conventions. It requires being attuned to the inherent authoritarian inclinations of vertical hierarchy so that you can avoid wielding power in domineering or disenfranchising ways.

Where it's necessary to take on leadership roles — because oftentimes thunderbolts are the wise choice, not only for dads, but also for everyone else — you'll need to leverage your power responsively. Prioritize listening over understanding so that you can be sure you're not alienating unfamiliar or historically pathologized voices. Rigorous inclusivity also involves always trying your best to avoid participating in systems that structurally reinforce stereotypes, prejudices, and presumptions — not only about men, women, and gender-nonconforming individuals, but also any and all other forms of sectarianism that lead to social exclusion.

Some people might argue that a parent's job is first and foremost to prepare children to succeed in the world as it is. Kids need to learn how to conform to the contextual realities they're bound to face even if we don't like how things are. Folks might argue that even though there's no scientific basis for gender essentialism, it's still a cultural reality and therefore we should equip our children with the tools necessary to thrive and fit into a world that's full of stereotypes. There are ways in which even this book aligns with that perspective. Despite knowing that there's no good argument for gender-specific parenting identities, I'm still analyzing and interpreting the father figure — and using he/him pronouns to do so — because I know that plenty of people adopt a dad persona and consider it to be inherently male. However, I also know that if I were to distinguish any specific fatherly traits and position them as primordially or eternally masculine, I'd be perpetuating the mythological fallacies of locker-room gender essentialism. Still, I've written this book primarily with cisgender men in mind, trying to equip them with feminist tools necessary to navigate the current cultural ethos. Why? Because a feminist dad needs to see his family (and all of his other relationships) as a microcosm of a more inclusive world. He needs to recognize that it's his duty to raise his children so that they're prepared to remake culture in a way that's rigorously and comprehensively inclusive.

To clarify what this looks like in everyday practice, I'll explain how I apply this same thinking in my college classroom. In addition to all the requisite academic content, I spend a few lessons each semester teaching students the skills involved in *listening mindfully* and *speaking with intention*. These are the skills at the heart of inclusivity. Listening mindfully has to do with critical consciousness. It requires witnessing. It's about avoiding the temptation to possess knowledge or to arrive at easy, tangible solutions. I remind students that most of the time we listen as if we're trying to geolocate a space where we can stake out our own intellectual territory. We ask: Do I agree or disagree? What can I take from this idea? How can I answer this question? Can this teacher offer cognitive assets of value? Is this classmate as smart as I am? Those are all examples of listening with authoritative intentions; you're trying to own and dominate the academic landscape. It's what Paulo Freire called "oppressor consciousness." Alternatively, listening mindfully means putting your raw experience of the discourse ahead of understanding, judging, or reaching a conclusion. To do so, you need to hear what others are saying and presume it represents something worthwhile, honorable, and dignified — even when the delivery sounds troublesome. You look beneath the surface and try to be attuned to an embedded truth. In other words, you're not listening for indicators and signifiers that tell you what baby-food jar the comment belongs in. Instead, you're validating all speakers by demonstrating your willingness to include their voices responsively.

Speaking with intention is the corollary—and especially when it comes to classrooms and business meetings, most of us stink at it. Have you ever raised your hand just to tell the group that you agree with a sentiment that's already been expressed? *I totally think the same thing, but I'd say it differently.* This is not an example of someone trying to contribute something new to the learning community, or the emergent discussion. Rather, it's an example of either trying to fortify your own position or reframing another person's thoughts so that they align with your narcissistic patriarchal authority. Guess what: Nobody needs to see it your way. That's not responsive; it's like asking someone's smartphone to automatically adjust to your website.

Instead, speaking with intention involves thinking about how your words will land and deeply considering whether they even need to be heard in the first place. Do they contribute anything to the collective conversation? There's no way to know—and no way to speak mindfully—unless you've already been listening with intention. This demonstrates inclusivity because it necessarily involves acknowledging that your voice is only one part of a participatory process of meaning-making. Yours is just one among many colliding myths. You can either contribute in a way that stakes out territory and puts up guard-rails, or you can let your voice build up the kind of platforms on which others can stand.

I always cover these ideas at the start of the semester, but then I try to revisit them later. Why? Because almost every-thing students have learned about how to engage with school — for at least twelve years before they arrive at university — teaches them the opposite: Don't practice mindful listening or intentional speech. We may tell them we value inclusivity (usually we call it diversity), but we do very little to teach them the skills involved in being inclusive. Instead, we promote a culture of rugged individual achievement.

Fatherhood is the same way. Dads may expound on the importance of diversity and inclusion, but we rarely teach our kids the skills necessary to enact the behaviors aligned with these values. When you think about that, it's shocking. Consider how much time fathers spend giving the kind of "dad-vice" that's typically associated with "masculinity." We teach our kids to throw a ball, to understand the rules of football or baseball, to handle power tools, to fix an engine. The media is full of aspirational images suggesting that the transmission of these practical everyday skills is at the foundation of what it means to be a good father figure. Yet we give almost no attention to the process of teaching the skills necessary for rigorous and comprehensive inclusivity.

A feminist dad knows better. He models rigorous inclusivity in every family interaction. He allows each voice to inform the dinner-table conversation equally. He values every reaction to the NPR story playing in the car — and even when it sounds dumb or immature, he probes for deeper meaning. This demonstrates that he knows there's a worthy voice hiding beneath every comment. He doesn't compete for attention; he welcomes partnership responsively. He also models a practice of individual psychological well-being that acknowledges we all have conflicting voices in our heads; he tells his children about his contradictory thoughts and feelings because he wants them to know that he's listening mindfully and speaking with intention even when it comes to an internal dialogue. He lets the skills of inclusivity inform everything he does.

CONCLUSION

FATHER FIGURE IN PROGRESS

SUNDAY, 8:22 A.M.: I usually drink my espresso from a clear, three-ounce Duralex glass—the kind you'd find in a French bistro. My kids never bought me one of those WORLD'S BEST DAD mugs. In fact, I don't think my kids would say that they have the world's best dad. I hope not. I'd want them to acknowledge that there are many things I could do better. That's why I've always been intentional about telling my kids that I make mistakes (they absolutely don't think I acknowledge it often enough). I also try to apologize to them when I lose my temper—which I do much more than I'd like. If everything goes according to plan, one day my kids will give me a mug that says, FATHER FIGURE IN PROGRESS.

I'm not being humble. I think I'm an awesome dad. In fact, if anyone deserves the world's greatest mug on Father's Day, it's me. It's not because I started my writing career as a video-game expert and gave my boys some of the coolest gamer experiences ever. No, it's because my kids have seen how often I'm engaged in a process of self-criticism. They recognize that I'm always trying to identify problematic cultural patterns, scripts, and structures that my habitual behaviors reproduce and maintain. I hope they're learning to associate that process with maturity. I consider myself a great dad because I think the image my kids have in their mind of what it looks like to be a mature man is a feminist dad.

I carry a tiny little imaginary action figure of my father in my pocket. He's like a Darth Vader or an Obi-Wan Kenobi toy — made of plastic, with articulating hip and shoulder joints. He speaks to me whenever I ask him to, like a superhero. He shows up especially in business meetings, or whenever I have to make financial decisions. He's often there when I'm negotiating — when I feel the need to demonstrate authority and power, when I want to project alpha-male confidence. He's a part of every ethical decision I make — I look to him whenever I wonder, *What's the right thing to do?* He's there watching over my home-improvement projects — plumbing, carpentry, or just hanging a framed photo. When I'm arguing or debating, he pops up to remind me to listen before I speak — because it's always better to play your cards after you see what your opponent has in their hand. He's there at the grocery-store freezer aisle, telling me to make sure the label says real "ice cream" and not phony "frozen dairy dessert." And because of him, I always put my kids first, even calling out from work if they need me; that's what Dad always did for me.

I'm glad to have him as a role model and adviser. I love my

dad and appreciate him more than you can possibly imagine, but my kids are growing up in a different world than I did, and I want to be a different kind of imaginary action figure in their pocket. I want them to see me as an image of critical consciousness, responsive fathering, anti–locker room gender essentialism, and rigorous inclusivity. I hope that when they're adults, they'll summon my voice when they struggle to contemplate the social and political implications of their actions.

I think this parenting thing is working out the way it should. My boys seem to look to me for answers to hard questions, at least some of the time. I also know that my students look to me for approval — sometimes I get emails from folks I taught years ago; they just want me to know that they're engaged in meaningful social-justice work. I puff my chest out with pride. I feel like I made a difference. I read their words to Amanda. And then self-doubt kicks in.

Father knows best? Inspirational professor? It bothers me that I remain in an authoritative position of power despite everything I do to deconstruct the sexist, misogynist, patriarchal behaviors we're all socialized to take for granted. I try so hard to model a different way of being, but there's no avoiding the privilege that society awards father figures. To pretend otherwise would make me complicit. Men have privilege. There's so much power in being a dad.

Dear fathers: I implore you, please wield that power in feminist ways.

To continue the conversation,
visit: www.FeministDadBook.com.

ACKNOWLEDGMENTS

Writing and researching this book has been much more arduous than I expected. I'm fortunate to have an exceptional editor: Tracy Behar. She has guided the process with noteworthy patience (and sometimes impatience). When I began working on this project in summer of 2019, I told Tracy that I needed to be free to follow the text to the most radical and extreme places it would go, while trusting that she'd reel it back in and help me refocus it when necessary. It was often necessary, and I always trusted her.

Thanks also to Jules, Jess, Ian, and all the other amazing folks at Little, Brown who have been so supportive of my work. Bonnie Solow is not only a fantastic literary agent but also a supportive friend, confidant, and adviser. She answers so many of my manic phone calls, responds calmly to my paranoia, cheers me on when I need it. Jazz Paquet read the penultimate draft of this book; their notes were both enlightening and emboldening.

ACKNOWLEDGMENTS

One night — a long time ago — at the diner, my friend Mac and I had a conversation about sex, gender, and identity. I was *so* wrong then. I've been trying to understand that look of scorn, contempt, and disbelief that they gave me ever since; now I think I get it.

George Papandreou consistently demonstrates to me that traditional notions of alpha-male power are not a prerequisite for meaningful leadership. Also, the personal stories he shared with me about working with Paulo Freire gave me the enthusiasm necessary to put critical consciousness at the core of this book.

Michael Stipe has been a friend, a role model, and an inspiration for almost two decades; it's hard to imagine I'd ever have written this book in the way that I did without his influence in my life.

A discussion I had with Ben Lee at the beginning of the writing process helped me understand it was imperative that I deconstruct Jungian gender essentialism in this book. Many conversations with Roxanne Partridge — especially one late-night argument at Aletis House about the nature of patriarchy — have informed the ideas on these pages. Robert Granat is an advocate for rigorous inclusivity with an especially cynical demeanor, which made him a great sounding board while dealing with some difficult editorial decisions. Frankie Tartaglia told me that books with yellow covers get the most attention. Jen Boulden screamed at me relentlessly until I arrived at a subtitle that met her approval. Meghan McDermott is always challenging, supporting, and celebrating my ideas. When Mary Watkins introduced me to community and liberation psychology, I didn't think I was interested; it has contoured all my work ever since. Ed Casey taught me how the tools of phenomenology can be pointed toward common social and political problems.

I'm grateful to all the students who have joined me in classrooms at Temple University; they consistently topple my expectations and assumptions, forcing me to reframe my thinking in more equitable and comprehensible ways. Ruth Ost and the rest of the honors program at Temple University greeted me almost every morning (pre-COVID-19), never complaining that I co-opted a desk in *their* space; I wrote the original proposal for this book at that desk. Douglas Greenfield, Dustin Kidd, Emily Carlin, and all my colleagues in the Intellectual Heritage Program continue to be a meaningful and supportive community.

Mom, Dad, Jessica, Courtney, the wise son, and the clever son — along with my nieces and nephews — constitute the best family imaginable. I'm lucky.

My children and my stepchildren deserve a thousand rewards for putting up with my stress and anxiety as this book's deadline approached, but I'm not giving them anything because they keep forgetting to put their dishes in the dishwasher.

Amanda is everything.

BIBLIOGRAPHY

Abramson, Kate. "Turning Up the Lights on Gaslighting." *Philosophical Perspectives*, vol. 28, no. 1, December 2014, 1–30.

Adams, Jimi and Ryan Light. "Scientific Consensus, the Law, and Same Sex Parenting Outcomes." *Social Science Research*, vol. 53, September 2015, 300–310.

Adams, Michael Vannoy. *The Mythological Unconscious*. London: Karnac Books, 2001.

Adichie, Chimamanda Ngozi. *Dear Ijeawele, or A Feminist Manifesto in Fifteen Suggestions*. New York: Knopf Doubleday, 2017.

—. *We Should All Be Feminists*. New York: Knopf Doubleday, 2014.

American Psychological Association, Boys and Men Guidelines Group. *APA Guidelines for Psychological Practice with Boys and Men*. 2018. apa. org/about/policy/psychological-practice-boys-men-guidelines.pdf

Aristotle. *Aristotle in 23 Volumes, Vol. 19,* translated by H. Rackham. Cambridge, MA: Harvard University Press; London: William Heinemann Ltd. 1934.

BIBLIOGRAPHY

Barker, Meg-John and Julia Scheele. *Queer: A Graphic History*. London: Icon, 2016.

Barthes, Roland. *Mythologies*. New York: Hill and Wang, 1972.

Batson, C. Daniel et al. "Empathic Joy and the Empathy-Altruism Hypothesis." *Journal of Personality and Social Psychology*, vol. 61, no. 3, 1991, 413–426.

Beck, Ulrich. "Democratization of the Family." *Childhood*, vol. 4, no. 2, 1997, 151–168.

Bernard, Tara Siegel. "When She Earns More: As Roles Shift, Old Ideas on Who Pays the Bills Persist." *New York Times*, July 6, 2018. nytimes.com/2018/07/06/your-money/marriage-men-women-finances.html

Black, Michael Ian. *A Better Man: A (Mostly Serious) Letter to My Son*. Chapel Hill, NC: Algonquin Books, 2020.

Blum-Ross, Alicia and Sonia Livingstone. *Parenting for a Digital Future: How Hopes and Fears about Technology Shape Children's Lives*. New York: Oxford University Press, 2020.

brown, adrienne maree. *Emergent Strategy: Shaping Change, Changing Worlds*. Chico, CA: AK Press, 2017.

Butler, Judith. *The Force of Non-Violence*. London: Verso, 2020.

Callard, Agnes. "Acceptance Parenting." *The Point*, October 2, 2020. thepointmag.com/examined-life/acceptance-parenting/

Campbell, Joseph. *The Hero With a Thousand Faces*. Princeton, NJ: Princeton University Press, 1949.

Carroll, Abigail. *Three Squares: The Invention of the American Meal*. New York: Basic Books, 2013.

Carroll, Noël. "Carlyle, Thomas." *Cambridge Dictionary of Philosophy*, edited by Robert Audi, 2nd ed., Cambridge University Press, 1999, p. 118.

BIBLIOGRAPHY

Center for Pew Research. "As Millennials Near 40, They're Approaching Family Life Differently Than Previous Generations." 2020.

—. "Marriage and Cohabitation in the US." 2019.

Cervantes, Miquel de. *Don Quixote: A New Translation by Edith Grossman.* Trans. Edith Grossman. New York: HarperCollins, 2003.

Chamorro-Premuzic, Tomas. *Why Do So Many Incompetent Men Become Leaders? (and how to fix it).* Boston, MA: Harvard Business Review Press, 2019.

Chilton, Bruce. *Christianity: The Basics.* London: Taylor & Francis, 2014.

—. *Rabbi Jesus.* New York: Bantam, 2000.

Coontz, Stephanie. *Marriage, a History: How Love Conquered Marriage.* New York: Penguin Publishing Group, 2006.

—. *The Way We Never Were: American Families and the Nostalgia Trip.* New York: Basic Books, 2016.

Covey, Stephen R. *The 7 Habits of Highly Effective People.* Miami, FL: Mango Media, 2015.

Coward, Rosalind. *Patriarchal Precedents: Sexuality and Social Relations.* London: Routledge & Kegan Paul, 1983.

Dancy, T. Elon. "Imposter Syndrome." In Kevin L. Nadal (ed.). *The SAGE Encyclopedia of Psychology and Gender.* Thousand Oaks, CA: SAGE Publications, 2017, 934–935.

Deaton, Jeremy, "Einstein Showed Newton Was Wrong about Gravity. Now Scientists Are Coming for Einstein." NBC News, August 3, 2019. nbcnews.com/mach/science/einstein-showed-newton-was-wrong -about-gravity-now-scientists-are-ncna1038671

D'Emilio, John. *Making Trouble: Essays on Gay History, Politics, and the University.* London: Routledge, 1992.

Dermott, Esther. *Intimate Fatherhood: A Sociological Analysis*. London: Routledge, 2008.

Derrida, Jacques. *Writing and Difference*. Chicago: University of Chicago Press, 2017.

Descartes, René. *Discourse on Method: Of Rightly Conducting One's Reason and of Seeking the Truth in The Sciences*. Auckland, New Zealand: Floating Press, 1924.

Devlin, Keith. *Goodbye Descartes: The End of Logic and the Search for a New Cosmology of the Mind*. New York: John Wiley & Sons, Inc., 1997.

Devlin, Rachel. *Relative Intimacy: Fathers, Adolescent Daughters, and Postwar American Culture*. Chapel Hill: University of North Carolina Press, 2005.

Elliott, Anthony. *Concepts of the Self*. Malden, MA: Polity, 2014.

Engels, Friedrich. *The Origin of Family, Private Property and the State*. London: Penguin Books Limited, 2010.

Faludi, Susan. *Stiffed: The Betrayal of the American Man*. New York: William Morrow and Company, Inc, 1999.

Fausto-Sterling, Anne. *Sex/Gender: Biology in a Social World*. London: Routledge, 2012.

Fine, Cordelia. *Testosterone rex: unmaking the myths of our gendered minds*. London: Icon, 2018.

Foucault, Michel. *The History of Sexuality: An Introduction*. New York: Vintage Books, 1990.

Frazer, James George. *Totemism and Exogamy*. New York: Cosimo Classics, 2010.

Freire, Paulo and Donaldo Macedo. *Pedagogy of the Oppressed 50th Anniversary Edition*. New York: Bloomsbury USA Academic, 2018.

Freire, Paulo. *Education for Critical Consciousness*. New York: Continuum, 1973.

BIBLIOGRAPHY

Freud, Sigmund. *Civilization and Its Discontents*. New York: W. W. Norton & Company, 2010.

Fuss, Diana. *Inside/Out: Lesbian Theories, Gay Theories*. London: Taylor & Francis, 1991.

Glynn, Adam, and Maya Sen. "Identifying Judicial Empathy: Does Having Daughters Cause Judges to Rule for Women's Issues?" *American Journal of Political Science*, vol. 59, no. 1, 37–54.

Goffman, Erving, Charles Lement, and Ann Branaman. *The Goffman Reader*. Malden, MA: Blackwell, 1997.

Gottlieb, Lori. *Maybe You Should Talk to Someone: A Therapist, Her Therapist, and Our Lives Revealed*. New York: Houghton Mifflin Harcourt, 2019.

Gray, John. *Men Are from Mars, Women Are from Venus: The Classic Guide to Understanding the Opposite Sex*. New York: Harper, 2012.

Green, Elliot. "What are the most-cited publications in the social sciences (according to Google Scholar)?" May 12, 2016. blogs.lse.ac.uk/impactof socialsciences/2016/05/12/what-are-the-most-cited-publications-in-the-social-sciences-according-to-google-scholar/

Griffin, Susan. *The Eros of Everyday Life: Essays on Ecology, Gender and Society*. New York: Doubleday, 1995.

Grimm, Jacob and Wilhelm Grimm. *Fairy Tales: The Complete Original Collection with Over 200 Stories*. Sudbury, MA: Ebookit.com, 2013.

Gutmann, Matthew. *Are Men Animals? How Modern Masculinity Sells Men Short*. New York: Basic Books, 2019.

Halberstam, Judith. *The Queer Art of Failure*. Durham: NC: Duke University Press, 2011.

Halperin, David. *One Hundred Years of Homosexuality and Other Essays on Greek Love*. New York: Routledge, 1990.

Hanh, Thich Nhat. *The Heart of the Buddha's Teaching: Transforming Suffering Into Peace, Joy, and Liberation*. New York: Potter/Ten Speed/ Rodale, 2015.

Harmon, Amy. "'They' Is the Word of the Year, Merriam-Webster Says, Noting Its Singular Rise." *New York Times*, December 10, 2019. nytimes.com/2019/12/10/us/merriam-webster-they-word-year.html

"Harper's Index." *Harper's Magazine,* January 2020.

Harris, Bud. *The Father Quest: Rediscovering An Elemental Psychic Force*. Alexander Books, 1996.

Hartocollis, Peter. "Origins and Evolution of the Oedipus Complex as Conceptualized by Freud." *Psychoanalytic Review,* vol. 92, no. 3, 315–334.

Headley, Maria Dahvana. *Beowulf: A New Translation*. New York: Farrar, Straus and Giroux, 2020.

Heidegger, Martin. *The Question Concerning Technology, and Other Essays*. Trans. William Lovitt. London: HarperCollins, 1977.

Heifitz, Ronald, Alexander Grashow, and Marty Linsky. *The Practice of Adaptive Leadership: Tools and Tactics for Changing Your Organization and the World*. Cambridge, MA: Harvard Business Press, 2009.

Hillman, James. *Mythic Figures*. Putnam, CT: Spring Publications, 2007.

—. *Re-Visioning Psychology*. New York: HarperCollins, 1992.

Homer. *Iliad*. London: Hackett Publishing, 1997.

—. *The Odyssey*. Trans. Emily Wilson. New York: W. W. Norton and Company, 2018.

hooks, bell. *Feminism Is for Everybody: Passionate Politics*. London: Pluto Press, 2000.

—. *Feminist Theory: From Margin to Center*. London: Taylor & Francis, 2014.

—. *The Will to Change: Men, Masculinity, and Love*. London: Atria Books, 2004.

Irigaray, Luce. *Speculum of the Other Woman*. Ithaca, NY: Cornell
    University Press, 1985.

Isaacson, Walter. *Steve Jobs*. New York: Simon & Schuster, 2011.

Jagose, Annamarie. *Queer Theory: An Introduction*. New York: New York
    University Press, 1996.

Joel, Daphna and Luba Vikhanski. *Gender Mosaic: Beyond the Myth of the
    Male and Female Brain*. New York: Little, Brown Spark, 2019.

Johnson, Eric Michael. "Raising Darwin's Consciousness: An Interview
    with Sarah Blaffer Hrdy on Mother Nature." *Scientific American,*
    March 16, 2012. blogs.scientificamerican.com/primate-diaries/raising
    -darwins-consciousness-an-interview-with-sarah-blaffer-hrdy-on
    -mother-nature/

Jordan-Young, Rebecca M. and Katrina Karkazis. *Testosterone: An Unauthorized
    Biography*. Cambridge, MA: Harvard University Press, 2019.

Joseph Campbell and the Power of Myth. Public Square Media, Inc., 1988.
    billmoyers.com/series/joseph-campbell-and-the-power-of-myth-1988/

Jung, Carl G. *Psychological Types*. Princeton, NJ: Princeton University
    Press, 1971.

—. *Two Essays on Analytical Psychology*. Princeton, NJ: Princeton
    University Press, 1977.

Kahn, Jack S. *An Introduction to Masculinities*. London: Wiley-Blackwell,
    2009.

Kamenetz, Anya. *The Art of Screen Time*. New York: PublicAffairs, 2018.

Kimmel, Michael. "Masculinity as Homophobia: Fear, Shame, and Silence in
    the Construction of Gender Identity." Brod, Harry and Michael Kimmel.
    Theorizing Masculinities. Newbury Park, CA: Sage, 1994. 119–141.

Kimmel, Michael S. *Manhood in America: A Cultural History*. Oxford:
    Oxford University Press, 2006.

Klasco, Richard. "Is There Such a Thing as a 'Sugar High'?" *New York Times*, February 25, 2020. nytimes.com/2020/02/21/well/eat/is-there -such-a-thing-as-a-sugar-high.html

Kuhn, Thomas S. *The Structure of Scientific Revolutions*. Chicago: University of Chicago Press, 1970.

Lamb, Michael E. *The Role of the Father in Child Development*. Fourth Edition. Hoboken, NJ: Wiley, 2004.

Lang, Gregory E., and Janet Lankford-Moran (illustrator). *Why a Daughter Needs a Dad* (miniature edition). New York: Sourcebooks, 2011.

Larson, Stephen and Robin Larson. *Joseph Campbell: A Fire in the Mind. The Authorized Biography*. Rochester, VT: Inner Traditions, 2002.

Lévi-Strauss, Claude. *The Savage Mind*. Chicago: University of Chicago Press, 1966.

Linton, David. *Men and Menstruation*. New York: Peter Lang, 2019.

Livingston, Gretchen and Kim Parker. "8 Facts about American Dads." June 12, 2019. *Pew Research Center*. pewresearch.org/fact-tank/2019/06 /12/fathers-day-facts/

Lockman, Darcy. *All The Rage: Mothers, Fathers, and the Myth of Equal Partnership*. New York: Harpers, 2019.

Long Chu, Andrea. *Females*. London: Verso, 2019.

Lupton, Deborah and Lesley Barclay. *Constructing Fatherhood*. London: SAGE Publications, 1997.

Machin, Anna. "How Men's Bodies Change When They Become Fathers." *New York Times: Parenting*, June 13, 2019. parenting.nytimes.com /health/fatherhood-mens-bodies?mcid=NYT&mc=EInternal&subid =Parenting&type=content

BIBLIOGRAPHY

Manne, Kate. *Down Girl: The Logic of Misogyny*. New York: Oxford University Press, 2019.

——. *Entitled: How Male Privilege Hurts Women*. New York: Crown, 2020.

Martin, Wednesday. *Untrue: Why Nearly Everything We Believe About Women, Lust, and Infidelity Is Wrong and How the New Science Can Set Us Free*. New York: Little, Brown Spark, 2018.

Massoni, Kelley. " 'Teena Goes to Market': *Seventeen* Magazine and the Early Construction of the Teen Girl (As) Consumer." *The Journal of American Culture*, vol. 29, no. 1, 31–42.

——. *Fashioning Teenagers: A Cultural History of* Seventeen *Magazine*. Walnut Creek, CA: Left Coast Press, 2010.

Milanich, Nara B. *Paternity: The Elusive Quest for the Father*. Cambridge, MA: Harvard University Press, 2019.

Moore, Robert and Douglas Gillette. *King, Warrior, Magician, Lover*. San Francisco: Harper, 1990.

Myers, Kyl. *Raising Them: Our Adventure in Gender Creative Parenting*. Amazon Publishing, 2020.

Nancy, Jean-Luc. *Listening*. New York: Fordham University Press, 2007.

Neumann, Erich. *The Great Mother: An Analysis of the Archetype*. Princeton, NJ: Bollingen/Princeton University Press, 1991.

Newman, Lucile. "The Couvade: A Reply to Kupferer." *American Anthropologist*, vol. 68, no. 1, 1966, new series, 153–156.

NPR. "Dad's YouTube Channel Advises How to Change a Flat, Other Life Skills." June 18, 2020. npr.org/2020/06/18/879892191/dads-youtube-channel-advises-how-to-change-a-flat-other-life-skills

Orenstein, Peggy. *Boys & Sex: Young Men on Hookups, Love, Porn, Consent, and Navigating the New Masculinity*. New York: Harper, 2020.

Orlinsky, Harry M. *The Torah: The Five Books of Moses*. Philadelphia, PA: Jewish Publication Society of America, 1967.

Otero, Solimar. ""Fearing our Mothers": An Overview of the Psychoanalytic Theories Concerning Vagina Dentata." *The American Journal of Psychoanalysis*, vol. 56, no. 3, 1996, 269.

Paglia, Camille. *Sexual Personae*. New Haven, CT: Yale University Press, 1990.

Paris, Ginette. *Pagan Meditations*. Woodstock, CT: Spring Publications, 1986.

Patterson, Jodie. *The Bold World: A Memoir of Family and Transformation*. New York: Ballantine, 2019.

Perris, Simon. "What Does Hine-Nui-Te-Pō Look Like? A Case Study of Oral Tradition, Myth, and Literature in Aotearoa New Zealand." *Journal of the Polynesian Society*, vol. 127, no. 4, 2018, 365–388.

Peterson, Jordan. *12 Rules for Life: An Antidote to Chaos*. New York: Random House, 2018.

Plank, Liz. *For the Love of Men: A New Vision of Mindful Masculinity*. New York: St. Martin's Press, 2019.

Plato. *Symposium*. Trans. Alexander Nehamas and Paul Woodruff. Indianapolis, IN: Hackett, 1989.

—. *The Trials of Socrates*. Trans. C. D. C. Reeve. Indianapolis, IN: Hackett, 2002.

Pruett, Kyle D. *Fatherneed: Why Father Care Is as Essential as Mother Care for Your Child*. New York: The Free Press, 2000.

Pugh, Allison. *Longing and Belonging: Parents, Children, and Consumer Culture*. Berkeley, CA: University of California Press, 2009.

Raeburn, Paul. *Do Fathers Matter? What Science Tells Us About the Parent We've Overlooked*. New York: Scientific American/Farrar, Straus and Giroux, 2014.

BIBLIOGRAPHY

Rankine, Claudia. *Just Us: An American Conversation*. Minneapolis, MN: Graywolf Press, 2020.

Real, Terrence. *How Can I Get Through to You: Closing the Intimacy Gap Between Men and Women*. New York: Fireside, 2002.

Ruhl, Sarah. *Eurydice*. New York: Samuel French, 2008.

Rushdie, Salman. *Quichotte*. New York: Random House, 2019.

Salam, Maya. "What Is Toxic Masculinity?" *New York Times*, January 22, 2019. nytimes.com/2019/01/22/us/toxic-masculinity.html

Sapolsky, Robert M. *The Trouble with Testosterone and Other Essays on the Biology of the Human Predicament*. New York: Scribner, 1997.

Sartre, Jean-Paul. *Basic Writings*. Ed. Stephen Priest. London: Routledge, 2001.

Sax, Leonard. "How Common Is Intersex? A Response to Anne Fausto-Sterling." *Journal of Sex Research*, vol. 39, no. 3, 2002, 174–178.

—.*Boys Adrift: The Five Factors Driving the Growing Epidemic of Unmotivated Boys and Underachieving Young Men*. New York: Basic Books, 2009.

Sears, Martha and William Sears. *The Attachment Parenting Book: A Commonsense Guide to Understanding and Nurturing Your Baby*. New York: Little, Brown, 2001.

Shapiro, Jordan. "Pulling Pork: Intimacy, Commitment, and Outdoor Cooking." *The Good Men Project*, July 10, 2013. goodmenproject. com/featured-content/pulling-pork-intimacy-commitment-and-outdoor-cooking/

—.*The New Childhood: Raising Kids to Thrive in a Connected World*. New York: Little, Brown Spark, 2018.

Sharrow, Elizabeth. "The First-Daughter Effect: The Impact of Fathering Daughters on Men's Preferences for Gender-Equality Policies." *Public Opinion Quarterly*, vol. 82, no. 3, 2018, 493–523.

Shulman, Helene and Mary Watkins. *Toward Psychologies of Liberation.* London: Palgrave Macmillan, 2008.

Shulster, Michael, Aaron M. Bernie, and Ranjith Ramasamy. "The Role of Estradiol in Male Reproductive Function." *Asian Journal of Andrology,* vol. 18, no. 3, May–June 2016, 434–440.

Solnit, Rebecca. *Men Explain Things to Me.* Chicago: Haymarket, 2014.

—. *Recollections of My Nonexistence.* New York: Viking, 2020.

—. *Whose Story Is This? Old Conflicts, New Chapters.* Chicago: Haymarket, 2019.

"SRY gene, sex determining region Y." Medline Plus, n.d. ghr.nlm.nih.gov/gene/SRY#conditions. Accessed February 4, 2020.

Stark, Cynthia A. "Gaslighting, Misogyny, and Psychological Oppression." *The Monist,* vol. 102, no. 2, 2019, 221.

Steinberg, Amanda. *Worth It: Your Life, Your Money, Your Terms.* New York: North Star Way, 2017.

Stolorow, Robert D. *World, Affectivity, Trauma: Heidegger and Post-Cartesian Psychoanalysis.* New York: Routledge, 2011.

Stueber, Karsten. "Empathy." In Edward N. Zalta (ed.). *The Stanford Encyclopedia of Philosophy.* Stanford, CA: Stanford University, 2017.

Swanson, Barrett. "Men at Work: Is There a Masculine Cure for Toxic Masculinity?" *Harper's Magazine,* November 2019, 22–33.

Tasker, Fiona. "Same-Sex Parenting and Child Development: Reviewing the Contribution of Parental Gender." *Journal of Marriage and Family,* vol. 72, no. 1, February 2010, 35–40.

UBS. "Own Your Worth." 2018.

Valdes, Francisco. "Unpacking Hetero-Patriarchy: Tracing the Conflation of Sex, Gender & Sexual Orientation to Its Origins." *Yale Journal of Law & the Humanities,* vol. 8, no. 1, 1996, 161–212.

Varbanova, Vladimira and John D. Hogan. "Deutsch, Helene." In: Robert W. Rieber R. (ed.), *Encyclopedia of the History of Psychological Theories.* New York: Springer, 2012.

Vernant, Jean-Pierre. *The Universe, the Gods, and Men: Ancient Greek Myths.* Trans. Linda Asher. New York: Perennial, 2002.

von Franz, Marie-Louise. *Puer Aeternus: A Psychological Study of the Adult Struggle with the Paradise of Childhood.* Boston, MA: Sigo Press, 1981.

—. *The Interpretation of Fairy Tales.* Boulder, CO: Shambhala, 1996.

Vonnegut, Kurt. *Mother Night.* New York: Dial Press, 2009.

Wallace, David Foster. *This Is Water: Some Thoughts, Delivered on a Significant Occasion, about Living a Compassionate Life.* New York: Little, Brown, 2009.

Ward, Jane. *The Tragedy of Heterosexuality.* New York: New York University Press, 2020.

Watkins, Mary. *Mutual Accompaniment and the Creation of the Commons.* New Haven, CT: Yale University Press, 2019.

West, Lindy. *The Witches Are Coming.* New York: Hachette Books, 2019.

Willingham, Emily. *Phallacy: Life Lessons from the Animal Penis.* New York: Penguin Publishing Group, 2020.

Wolraich, Mark L., David B. Wilson, and J. Wade White. "The Effect of Sugar on Behavior or Cognition in Children. A Meta-analysis." *Journal of the American Medical Association*, vol. 274, no. 20, 1995, 1617–1621.

Women's Media Center. *Divided 2019: The Media Gender Gap.* January 31, 2019. womensmediacenter.com/reports/divided-2019-the-media-gender-gap

Zoja, Luigi. *The Father: Historical, Psychological and Cultural Perspectives.* Trans. Henry Martin. London: Banner-Routledge, 2001.

Zuckerberg, Donna. *Not All Dead White Men: Classics and Misogyny in the Digital Age.* Cambridge, MA: Harvard University Press, 2018.

NOTES

INTRODUCTION

1. Coontz, Stephanie. *The Way We Never Were: American Families and the Nostalgia Trap.* New York: Basic Books, 2016.

2. hooks, bell. *Feminism Is for Everybody: Passionate Politics.* London: Pluto Press, 2000.

3. Adichie, Chimamanda Ngozi. *We Should All Be Feminists.* New York: Knopf Doubleday Publishing Group, 2014.

4. hooks, bell. *Feminist Theory: From Margin to Center.* Abingdon: Taylor & Francis, 2014.

5. I'm a cisgendered man. I prefer not to identify as gay or straight, as I believe people love people, not labels. For most of my adult life, I've used the word *queer* because it's noncategorical and therefore more inclusive, but I've been in a long-term heterosexual relationship with a woman (Amanda) for almost a decade. I was birthed into a Judaic household—I say *Judaic* rather than *Jewish* because I consider Judaism to be a religion and a culture, rather than a biological or genetic category.

Still, most people would consider me to be "Jewish." Of course, there's a question about whether "Jews" are "white," so it's complicated for me to identify as a white male. Nevertheless, my skin is pale and I benefit from white, male, cisgender, and heterosexual privilege.

6. Shapiro, Jordan. "Pulling Pork: Intimacy, Commitment, and Outdoor Cooking." *The Good Men Project.* July 19, 2013. goodmenproject .com/featured-content/pulling-pork-intimacy-commitment-and -outdoor-cooking/

7. This example is borrowed from Myers, Kyl. *Raising Them: Our Adventure in Gender Creative Parenting.* Amazon Publishing, 2020.

8. hooks, bell. *The Will to Change: Men, Masculinity, and Love.* New York: Atria Books, 2004.

9. Adichie, Chimamanda Ngozi. *Dear Ijeawele, or A Feminist Manifesto in Fifteen Suggestions.* New York: Knopf Doubleday, 2017.

PART ONE

1. Vonnegut, Kurt. *Mother Night.* New York: Dial Press, 2009.

2. Jung, Carl G. *Psychological Types,* vol. 6. Princeton, NJ: Princeton University Press, 1971. (Paragraph 803)

3. Jung, Carl G. *Two Essays on Analytical Psychology.* Princeton, NJ: Princeton University Press, 1977. (Paragraph 305)

4. Green, Elliot. "What are the most-cited publications in the social sciences (according to Google Scholar)?" May 12, 2016. blogs.lse.ac.uk/ impactofsocialsciences/2016/05/12/what-are-the-most-cited-publications -in-the-social-sciences-according-to-google-scholar/

5. Goffman, Erving, Charles Lement, and Ann Branaman. *The Goffman Reader.* Malden, MA: Blackwell, 1997.

6. Although not a direct quote, I've borrowed this "cause and effect" phrasing from Anthony Elliot, *Concepts of the Self*. Malden, MA: Polity, 2014.

7. See Taylor Swift's 2020 Netflix documentary *Taylor Swift: Miss Americana*, in which she says, "You become the person they want you to be."

8. Raeburn, Paul. *Do Fathers Matter? What Science Tells Us About the Parent We've Overlooked*. New York: Scientific American/Farrar, Straus and Giroux, 2014.

9. Machin, Anna. "How Men's Bodies Change When They Become Fathers." *New York Times: Parenting*, June 13, 2019. parenting.nytimes .com/health/fatherhood-mens-bodies?mcid=NYT&mc=EInternal&subid =Parenting&type=content

10. Raeburn. *Do Fathers Matter?*

11. Newman, Lucile. "The Couvade: A Reply to Kupferer." *American Anthropologist*, vol. 68, no. 1, 1966, new series, 153–156.

12. Newman, Barbara and Leslie Newman. "Some Birth Customs in East Anglia." *Folklore*, vol. 50, no. 2, 1939, 176–187.

13. Frazer, James George. *Totemism and Exogamy*. New York: Cosimo Classics, 2010.

14. Tasker, Fiona. "Same-Sex Parenting and Child Development: Reviewing the Contribution of Parental Gender. *Journal of Marriage and Family*, vol. 72, no. 1, February 2010, 35–40.

15. Adams, Jimi and Ryan Light. "Scientific Consensus, the Law, and Same Sex Parenting Outcomes." *Social Science Research*, vol. 53, September 2015, 300–310.

16. hooks, bell. *Feminism Is for Everybody: Passionate Politics*. London: Pluto Press, 2000.

17. Manne, Kate. *Entitled: How Male Privilege Hurts Women*. New York: Crown, 2020.

18. "The Benefits of Babywearing, Learning Different Carries, and More." Attachment Parenting International. attachmentparenting.org/parenting topics/infants-toddlers/babywearingtouch

19. Sears, Martha and William Sears. *The Attachment Parenting Book: A Commonsense Guide to Understanding and Nurturing Your Baby*. New York: Little, Brown, 2001. Chapter 6, "Babywearing."

20. All the statistics in this paragraph come from: Livingston, Gretchen and Kim Parker. "8 Facts about American Dads." June 12, 2019. Pew Research Center. pewresearch.org/fact-tank/2019/06/12/fathers-day-facts/

21. Ibid.

22. Harmon, Amy. " 'They' Is the Word of the Year, Merriam-Webster Says, Noting Its Singular Rise." *New York Times*, December 10, 2019. nytimes. com/2019/12/10/us/merriam-webster-they-word-year.html

23. See "Introduction: They Let You Do it" in West, Lindy. *The Witches Are Coming*. New York: Hachette, 2019.

24. I write about this resistance to family change in detail in *The New Childhood*. See: "Part Two: Home" in Shapiro, Jordan. *The New Childhood: Raising Kids to Thrive in a Connected World*. New York: Little, Brown, 2018.

25. Certainly, there are many historic and prehistoric examples of social roles being divided according to gender, but this particular one would have seemed absurd to premodern humans. As historian Stephanie Coontz explains, the 1950s were the first time "a majority of marriages in Western Europe and North America consisted of a full-time homemaker supported by a male earner." The mid-twentieth century is the only time in history that the majority of families could "actually

survive on the earnings of a single breadwinner." See: Coontz, Stephanie. *Marriage, a History: How Love Conquered Marriage.* New York: Penguin Publishing Group, 2006.

26. Kimmel, Michael. "Masculinity as Homophobia: Fear, Shame, and Silence in the Construction of Gender Identity." In M. M. Gergen and S. N. Davis (eds.), *Toward a New Psychology of Gender*, Abingdon: Taylor & Francis, 1997, 223–242. Brod, Harry and Michael Kimmel. *Theorizing Masculinities.* Newbury Park, CA: Sage, 1994. 119–141.

27. Coontz, Stephanie. *The Way We Never Were: American Families and the Nostalgia Trap.* New York: Basic Books, 2016.

28. Salam, Maya. "What Is Toxic Masculinity?" *New York Times*, January 22, 2019. nytimes.com/2019/01/22/us/toxic-masculinity.html

29. American Psychological Association, Boys and Men Guidelines Group. *APA Guidelines for Psychological Practice with Boys and Men.* 2018. apa. org/about/policy/psychological-practice-boys-men-guidelines.pdf

30. "Of course, it's breathtakingly naïve to think that therapy alone would be enough to redress the larger systemic forces behind a problem like toxic masculinity," journalist Barrett Swanson wrote in *Harper's Magazine,* after spending the weekend engaged in "manhood-confirming adventures" at an upscale nature lodge in Ohio. See: Swanson, Barrett. "Men at Work: Is There a Masculine Cure for Toxic Masculinity?" *Harper's Magazine*, November 2019: 22–33.

31. Hartocollis, Peter. "Origins and Evolution of the Oedipus Complex as Conceptualized by Freud." *Psychoanalytic Review*, vol. 92, no. 3, 315–334.

32. Larson, Stephen and Robin Larson. *Joseph Campbell: A Fire in the Mind. The Authorized Biography.* Rochester, Vermont: Inner Traditions, 2002.

33. *Joseph Campbell and the Power of Myth*. Public Square Media, Inc., 1988. billmoyers.com/series/joseph-campbell-and-the-power-of-myth-1988/

34. Campbell uses the term *Mystagogue* throughout this section, a term that originally referred to the folks who initiated candidates into the ancient Eleusinian Mysteries.

35. His emphasis, not mine.

36. Headley, Maria Dahvana. *Beowulf: A New Translation.* New York: Farrar, Straus and Giroux, 2020.

37. Vernant, Jean-Pierre. *The Universe, the Gods, and Men: Ancient Greek Myths.* Trans. Linda Asher. New York: Perennial, 2002.

38. Black, Michael Ian. *A Better Man: A (Mostly Serious) Letter to My Son.* Chapel Hill, NC: Algonquin Books, 2020.

39. "It is startling to realize that the Lord's Prayer, which Christian teachers (and even scholars) have claimed is unique, derives from the Qaddish." See: Chilton, Bruce. *Rabbi Jesus.* New York: Bantam, 2000.

40. Gutmann, Matthew. *Are Men Animals? How Modern Masculinty Sells Men Short.* New York: Basic Books, 2019.

41. Of course, this framework also plays a crucial role in enabling the psychological well-being (and human rights) of gender-nonconforming individuals who have suffered because of the traditional binary male/female categories.

42. Fausto-Sterling, Anne. *Sex/Gender: Biology in a Social World.* London: Routledge, 2012.

43. Sax, Leonard. "How Common Is Intersex? A Response to Anne Fausto-Sterling." *Journal of Sex Research*, vol. 39, no. 3, August 2002, 174–178.

44. This explanation of why sex is a spectrum has shown up in many Twitter threads, too many to know who composed it first. For instance, see: twitter.com/ScienceVet2/status/1035246030500061184?s=20 and twitter.com/RebeccaRHelm/status/1207834357639139328?s=20. After doing rigorous research to confirm the facts, I decided that the original rhetorical

structure found on Twitter worked best. I've paraphrased, rephrased, combined multiple threads, made some additions and subtractions. But I don't deserve full credit for the rhetorical construction of this argument.

45. Is this really how SRY is expected to behave? Note that this careless phrasing presumes a "normal" version of sexual biology.

46. "SRY gene, sex determining region Y." Medline Plus, n.d. ghr.nlm.nih .gov/gene/SRY#conditions. Accessed February 4, 2020.

47. "Estradiol in men is essential for modulating libido, erectile function, and spermatogenesis. Estrogen receptors, as well as aromatase, the enzyme that converts testosterone to estrogen, are abundant in brain, penis, and testis, organs important for sexual function. In the brain, estradiol synthesis is increased in areas related to sexual arousal. In addition, in the penis, estrogen receptors are found throughout the corpus cavernosum with high concentration around neurovascular bundles." Shulster, Michael, Aaron M. Bernie, and Ranjith Ramasamy. "The Role of Estradiol in Male Reproductive Function." *Asian Journal of Andrology*, vol. 18, no. 3, May–June 2016, 434–440.

48. Jordan-Young, Rebecca M. and Katrina Karkazis. *Testosterone: An Unauthorized Biography*. Cambridge, MA: Harvard University Press, 2019.

49. Fine, Cordelia. *Testosterone rex: Unmaking the Myths of Our Gendered Minds*. London: Icon, 2018.

50. I don't mean to exclude adoptive fathers here. I'm just referencing my own circumstances, not implying that this is a defining characteristic of fatherhood.

51. Moore, Robert and Douglas Gillette. *King, Warrior, Magician, Lover*. San Francisco: Harper, 1990.

52. Peterson, Jordan B. *12 Rules for Life: An Antidote to Chaos*. Toronto: Penguin Random House, 2018.

53. Barthes, Roland. *Mythologies*. New York: Hill and Wang, 1972. Preface, page 10.

54. Ibid.

55. Credit is due to Lori Gottlieb, author of *Maybe You Should Talk to Someone*, for the "unreliable narrator" phrasing.

PART TWO

1. Iris Smyles is the author I'm referring to here. Her books are great. I recommend them.

2. According to the mythology, Hera brought forth Hephaistos without any help from Zeus. The crippled god of the forge might be better characterized as Zeus's stepson.

3. *Iliad*. Cambridge, MA: Hackett Publishing, 1997. Book 18, Lines 504–559.

4. Hillman, James. *Re-Visioning Psychology*. New York: HarperCollins, 1992.

5. Hanh, Thich Nhat. *The Heart of the Buddha's Teaching: Transforming Suffering Into Peace, Joy, and Liberation*. New York: Potter/Ten Speed/Harmony/Rodale, 2015.

6. Hillman, James. *Re-Visioning Psychology*. New York: HarperCollins, 1992.

7. Adams, Michael Vannoy. *The Mythological Unconscious*. London: Karnac Books, 2001.

8. "Look at the word responsibility — 'response-ability' — the ability to choose your response." Covey, Stephen R. *The 7 Habits of Highly Effective People*. Miami, FL: Mango Media, 2015.

9. Hall of Fame defensive end Deacon Jones said, "Dick was an animal. I called him a maniac. A stone maniac. He was a well-conditioned animal, and every time he hit you, he tried to put you in the cemetery, not the hospital." nbcsports.com/chicago/chicago-bears/bears-classics-dick -butkus-profiles-standard-mlb-greatness

NOTES

10. Willingham, Emily. *Phallacy: Life Lessons from the Animal Penis*. New York: Penguin Publishing Group, 2020.

11. Maybe even more than "everything under the sun," but this was the time before heliocentrism was accepted as fact.

12. In fact, this is exactly what happened until Einstein's theory of relativity displaced Newton's description of gravity. Einstein's theory changed our understanding of gravity. It went from a simple, mechanical, attractive force, to the curve of space and time around an object. Now, physicists recognize that black holes challenge the authority of Einstein's theory. See Deaton, Jeremy, "Einstein Showed Newton Was Wrong about Gravity. Now Scientists Are Coming for Einstein." NBC News, August 3, 2019. nbcnews.com/mach/science/einstein-showed-newton-was-wrong-about-gravity-now-scientists-are-ncna1038671

13. Orlinsky, Harry M. *The Torah: The Five Books of Moses*. Philadelphia, PA: Jewish Publication Society of America, 1967.

14. See John Stuart Mill and Harry Frankfurt for other influential accounts of "autonomy." Mill makes space for bodily desires and instincts — provided a person is directing their own actions. Frankfurt lays out a hierarchal view of autonomy with first-order desires being reflexively endorsed by second-order desires.

15. Franz, Marie-Luise von. *The Interpretation of Fairy Tales*. Boulder, CO: Shambhala, 1996.

16. Engels, Friedrich. *The Origin of the Family, Private Property and the State*. London: Penguin Books Limited, 2010.

17. Grimm, Jacob and Wilhelm Grimm. *Fairy Tales: The Complete Original Collection with Over 200 Stories*. Sudbury, MA: Ebookit.com, 2013.

18. Franz. *The Interpretation of Fairy Tales*.

19. Ibid.

20. See "Einstein's Brain" in Barthes, Roland. *Mythologies*. New York: Hill and Wang, 1972.

21. Kuhn, Thomas S. *The Structure of Scientific Revolutions*. Chicago: University of Chicago Press, 1962.

22. Manne, Kate. *Down Girl: The Logic of Misogyny*. New York: Oxford University Press, 2019.

23. Franz. *The Interpretation of Fairy Tales*.

24. Pew Research Center. "Marriage and Cohabitation in the U.S." November 2019.

25. Coontz, Stephanie. *Marriage, a History: How Love Conquered Marriage*. New York: Penguin Publishing Group, 2006.

26. Abramson, Kate. "Turning Up the Lights on Gaslighting." *Philosophical Perspectives*, vol. 28, no. 1, December 2014, 1–30.

27. Manne. *Down Girl*.

28. Stark, Cynthia A. "Gaslighting, Misogyny, and Psychological Oppression." *The Monist*, vol. 102, no. 2, 2019, 221–235.

29. Descartes, René. *Discourse on Method: Of Rightly Conducting One's Reason and of Seeking Truth in the Sciences*. Auckland, New Zealand: Floating Press, 1924.

30. Thomas Carlyle laid out this view in his 1841 book, *On Heroes, Hero-Worship and the Heroic in History*. "Universal History, the history of what man has accomplished in this world, is at bottom the History of the Great Men who have worked here. They were the leaders of men, these great ones; the modellers, patterns, and in a wide sense creators, of whatsoever the general mass of men contrived to do or to attain; all things that we see standing accomplished in the world are properly the outer material result, the practical realisation and embodiment, of

thoughts that dwelt in the Great Men sent into the world: the soul of the whole world's history, it may justly be considered, were the history of these." See: Carroll, Noël. "Carlyle, Thomas." *Cambridge Dictionary of Philosophy*, edited by Robert Audi, 2nd ed., Cambridge University Press, 1999, 118. Carlyle's view of history has been challenged and mostly rejected by historians. But I'd argue most of us continue to unconsciously ascribe to it.

31. Cervantes, Miguel de. *Don Quixote.* New York: HarperCollins, 2003.

32. Isaacson, Walter. *Steve Jobs.* New York: Simon & Schuster, 2011.

33. I'm paraphrasing Roland Barthes here. Actually, I'm carelessly mashing together the two phrases I quoted in part one: "How It's Always Been."

34. brown, adrienne maree. *Emergent Strategy: Shaping Change, Changing Worlds.* Chico, CA: AK Press, 2017.

35. Interestingly, the term *imposter syndrome* came from a study of women college students and faculty who "felt internally fraudulent and stressed about their abilities despite high levels of achievement." Dancy, T. Elon. "Impostor Syndrome." *The SAGE Encyclopedia of Psychology and Gender.* Ed. Kevin L. Nadal. Thousand Oaks, CA: SAGE Publications, Inc., 2017, 934–935.

36. Hanh, Thich Nhat. *The Heart of the Buddha's Teaching: Transforming Suffering Into Peace, Joy, and Liberation.* New York: Potter/Ten Speed/Harmony/Rodale, 2015.

PART THREE

1. Klasco, Richard. "Is There Such a Thing as a 'Sugar High'?" *New York Times*, February 25, 2020. nytimes.com/2020/02/21/well/eat/is-there-such-a-thing-as-a-sugar-high.html

2. Carroll, Abigail. *Three Squares: The Invention of the American Meal*. New York: Basic Books, 2013.

3. Wolraich, Mark L., David B. Wilson, and J. Wade White. "The Effect of Sugar on Behavior or Cognition in Children. A Meta-analysis." *Journal of the American Medical Association*, vol. 274, no. 20, 1995, 1617–1621.

4. Aristotle. *Aristotle in 23 Volumes, Vol. 19*, translated by H. Rackham. Cambridge, MA: Harvard University Press; London: William Heinemann Ltd. 1934.

5. In Plato's *Symposium*, Socrates says, "The only thing I say I understand is the art of love." It's a play on words, emphasizing the similarity between the noun *erôs* ("love") and the verb *erôtan* ("to ask questions"). He's also hinting at the idea that eros tends to involve probing and uncovering.

6. Devlin, Rachel. *Relative Intimacy: Fathers, Adolescent Daughters, and Postwar American Culture*. Chapel Hill, NC: University of North Carolina Press, 2005.

7. Varbanova, Vladimira and John D. Hogan. "Deutsch, Helene." In: Robert W. Rieber R. (ed.), *Encyclopedia of the History of Psychological Theories*. New York: Springer, 2012.

8. Devlin. *Relative Intimacy*.

9. Massoni, Kelley. " 'Teena Goes to Market': *Seventeen* Magazine and the Early Construction of the Teen Girl (As) Consumer." *The Journal of American Culture*, vol. 29, no. 1, 31–42.

10. Ibid.

11. Massoni, Kelley. *Fashioning Teenagers: A Cultural History of* Seventeen *Magazine*. Walnut Creek, CA: Left Coast Press, 2010.

12. While daddy–daughter eros wasn't supposed to be incestuous, many case histories suggest that some doctors practicing at the time considered

a consummated sexual encounter between a father and his daughter to be less worrisome, less likely to muck up a healthy Oedipal Stage 2.0, than no relationship at all. See: Devlin, Rachel. *Relative Intimacy: Fathers, Adolescent Daughters, and Postwar American Culture*. Chapel Hill, NC: University of North Carolina Press, 2005.

13. See Rachel Devlin's discussion of Edward Streeter's *The Father of the Bride*, published in 1948, and the movie adaptation of 1950. "Dating back to at least the eighteenth century, the ritual of the father walking the bride to meet her groom was, by 1948, well established. However, the singular attention to the various responsibilities and emotional quandaries of the *father* associated with the ceremony itself represented a new point of interest in the wedding, one that emerged virtually overnight with the publication of Streeter's book." See: Devlin. *Relative Intimacy*.

14. Ruhl, Sarah. *Eurydice*. New York: Samuel French, 2008.

15. Lang, Gregory E. and Janet Lankford-Moran (illustrator). *Why a Daughter Needs a Dad* (miniature edition). New York: Sourcebooks, 2011.

16. Homer. *The Odyssey*. New York: W. W. Norton, 2017.

17. See: Johnson, Eric Michael. "Raising Darwin's Consciousness: An Interview with Sarah Blaffer Hrdy on Mother Nature." *Scientific American,* March 16, 2012. blogs.scientificamerican.com/primate-diaries /raising-darwins-consciousness-an-interview-with-sarah-blaffer -hrdy-on-mother-nature/

18. Adichie, Chimamanda Ngozi. *Dear Ijeawele, or A Feminist Manifesto in Fifteen Suggestions*. New York: Knopf Doubleday Publishing Group, 2017.

19. Blum-Ross, Alicia and Sonia Livingstone. *Parenting for a Digital Future: How Hopes and Fears about Technology Shape Children's Lives*. New York: Oxford University Press, 2020.

20. Beck, Ulrich. "Democratization of the Family." *Childhood*, vol. 4, no. 2, 1997, 151–168.

21. Callard, Agnes. "Acceptance Parenting." *The Point*, October 2, 2020. thepointmag.com/examined-life/acceptance-parenting/

22. Beck, Ulrich. "Democratization of the Family." *Childhood*, vol. 4, no. 2, 1997, 151–168.

23. I borrowed the language *symbolic deprivation* and *symbolic indulgence* from Allison Pugh, who uses it to describe how socioeconomic status impacts child-rearing practices. See: Pugh, Allison. *Longing and Belonging: Parents, Children, and Consumer Culture*. Berkeley, CA: University of California Press, 2009.

24. UBS. "Own Your Worth." 2018. ubs.com/content/dam/WealthManagementAmericas/documents/2018-37666-UBS-Own-Your-Worth-report-R32.pdf

25. Bernard, Tara Siegel. "When She Earns More: As Roles Shift, Old Ideas on Who Pays the Bills Persist." *New York Times*, July 6, 2018. nytimes.com/2018/07/06/your-money/marriage-men-women-finances.html

26. Batson, C. Daniel et al. "Empathic Joy and the Empathy-Altruism Hypothesis." *Journal of Personality and Social Psychology*, vol. 61, no. 3, 1991, 413–426.

27. See my previous book, *The New Childhood: Raising Kids to Thrive in a Connected World*, for a more comprehensive discussion of the problems with "empathy."

28. Sharrow, Elizabeth A. et al. "The First-Daughter Effect: The Impact of Fathering Daughters on Men's Preferences for Gender-Equality Policies." *Public Opinion Quarterly*, vol. 82, no. 3, Fall 2018, 493–523.

29. Glynn, Adam and Maya Sen. "Identifying Judicial Empathy: Does Having Daughters Cause Judges to Rule for Women's Issues?" *American Journal of Political Science*, vol. 59, no. 1, 37–54.

30. Sharrow, et al. "The First-Daughter Effect."

31. Myers, Kyl. *Raising Them: Our Adventure in Gender Creative Parenting.* Amazon Publishing, 2020.

32. Manne, Kate. *Down Girl: The Logic of Misogyny.* Oxford: Oxford University Press, 2018.

33. During his confirmation process, then U.S. Supreme Court nominee Brett Kavanaugh told members of the Senate Judiciary Committee about coaching his daughters' basketball teams. In his opening statement he said, "I love coaching more than anything I've ever done in my life. But thanks to what some of you on this side of the committee have unleashed, I may never be able to coach again." usatoday.com/story/sports /columnist/erik-brady/2018/09/28/brett-wwwright-he-can-no-longer -coach-girls-basketball/1459496002/

34. As Kate Manne explains, "It's not obvious on the face of it that Trump has especially sexist beliefs about women's (in)ability to compete with him in business and politics at his own level (such as it is). For one thing, Trump employs women in high-powered positions in his companies, which suggests he doesn't underestimate (all) women—rather, he needs to control them, and head off the risk of their outshining him." Manne, Kate. *Down Girl: The Logic of Misogyny.* Oxford: Oxford University Press, 2018.

35. Pew Research Center. "As Millennials Near 40, They're Approaching Family Life Differently Than Previous Generations." May 2020.

36. Lockman, Darcy. *All the Rage: Mothers, Fathers, and the Myth of Equal Partnership.* New York: Harper, 2019.

37. My friend and colleague Anya Kamenetz once adroitly suggested that most of the differences between our respective books on children and screen time make sense when viewed through this lens of gender roles: She offers moms a way to plan for more balance, whereas I suggest, from a father's perspective, that everyone should play more video games with their kids. See: Kamenetz, Anya. *The Art of Screen Time: How Your Family Can Balance Digital Media and Real Life*. New York: PublicAffairs, 2018.

38. Shapiro, Jordan. "Pulling Pork: Intimacy, Commitment, and Outdoor Cooking." *The Good Men Project*. July 10, 2013. goodmenproject.com/featured-content/pulling-pork-intimacy-commitment-and-outdoor-cooking/

39. For a fantastic account of the construction of "heterosexuality" and opposite-sex relationships built on the mythology of "mutual affection," see: Ward, Jane. *The Tragedy of Heterosexuality*. New York: New York University Press, 2020.

40. Valdes, Francisco. "Unpacking Hetero-Patriarchy: Tracing the Conflation of Sex, Gender & Sexual Orientation to Its Origins." *Yale Journal of Law & the Humanities,* vol. 8, no. 1, Winter 1996, 161–212.

41. Joel, Daphna and Luba Vikhanski. *Gender Mosaic: Beyond the Myth of the Male and Female Brain*. New York: Little, Brown Spark, 2019.

42. Myers, Kyl. *Raising Them: Our Adventure in Gender Creative Parenting*. Amazon Publishing, 2020.

43. Neumann, Erich. *The Great Mother: An Analysis of the Archetype*. Princeton, NJ: Princeton University Press, 2015.

44. Hanly, Patrick and Anthony Alpers. *Maori Myths & Tribal Legends*. London: J. Murray, 1964.

45. "During the development of *Moana*, the volcanic goddess Te Kā ('Blazing', 'Burning') was originally named Te Pō ('Night', 'Darkness')

in reference to Hine-nui-te-pō." See: Perris, Simon. "What Does Hine-Nui-Te-Pō Look Like? A Case Study of Oral Tradition, Myth, and Literature in Aotearoa New Zealand." *Journal of the Polynesian Society*, vol. 127, no. 4, 2018, 365–388.

46. Paglia, Camille. *Sexual Personae*. New Haven, CT: Yale University Press, 1990.

47. Irigaray, Luce. *Speculum of the Other Woman*. Ithaca, NY: Cornell University Press, 1985.

48. Gray, John. *Men Are from Mars, Women Are from Venus: The Classic Guide to Understanding the Opposite Sex*. New York: Harper, 2012.

PART FOUR

1. Martin Heidegger wrote, "That which gives bounds, that which completes, in this sense is called in Greek *telos*, which is all too often translated as 'aim' or 'purpose,' and so misinterpreted." Lovitt, William and Martin Heidegger. *The Question Concerning Technology, and Other Essays*. New York: HarperCollins, 1977.

2. "There are these two young fish swimming along, and they happen to meet an older fish swimming the other way, who nods at them and says, 'Morning, boys. How's the water?' And the two young fish swim on for a bit, and then eventually one of them looks over at the other and goes, 'What the hell is water?'" Wallace, David Foster. *This Is Water: Some Thoughts, Delivered on a Significant Occasion, about Living a Compassionate Life*. New York: Little, Brown, 2009.

3. Campbell, Joseph. *The Hero with a Thousand Faces*. Novato, CA: New World Library, 2008.

4. Freire, Paulo. *Pedagogy of the Oppressed: 50th Anniversary Edition*. New York: Bloomsbury Publishing, 2018.

5. Ibid.

6. Freire, Paulo et al. *Education for Critical Consciousness*. New York: Continuum, 1973.

7. Shulman, Helene and Mary Watkins. *Toward Psychologies of Liberation*. London: Palgrave Macmillan UK, 2008.

8. hooks, bell. *The Will to Change: Men, Masculinity, and Love*. New York: Atria Books, 2004.

9. Kimmel, Michael. "Masculinity as Homophobia: Fear, Shame, and Silence in the Construction of Gender Identity." In Harry W. Brod and Michael Kaufman (eds.), *Research on Men and Masculinities Series: Theorizing Masculinities*. Thousand Oaks, CA: SAGE Publications, Inc., 119–141.

10. I'm paraphrasing Roland Barthes here…again, carelessly mashing together the two phrases I quoted in part one:, "How It's Always Been."

11. Psychologist and bestselling author Leonard Sax writes that the "devaluation and disintegration of the masculine ideal" is one of five primary factors hurting boys in today's culture. *Ugh!!* To make matters worse, he names the chapter in which he describes it "The Revenge of the Forsaken Gods." He seems to be implying that shifting our understanding of manhood is a violation of the natural, ancient, primordial God-given order of things. It's a clear and jarring example of locker-room gender essentialism. See: Sax, Leonard. *Boys Adrift: The Five Factors Driving the Growing Epidemic of Unmotivated Boys and Underachieving Young Men*. New York: Basic Books, 2016.

12. Nancy, Jean-Luc et al. *Listening*. New York: Fordham University Press, 2007.

NOTES

13. NPR. "Dad's YouTube Channel Advises How to Change a Flat, Other Life Skills." June 18, 2020. npr.org/2020/06/18/879892191/dads-youtube -channel-advises-how-to-change-a-flat-other-life-skills

14. The anthropologist Claude Lévi-Strauss describes Bricoleur this way: "His universe of instruments is closed and the rules of his game are always to make do with 'whatever is at hand,' that is to say with a set of tools and materials which is always finite and is also heterogeneous because what it contains bears no relation to the current project, or indeed to any particular project." Lévi-Strauss is talking about mythological thought. He's describing the way narratives and identities are constructed by combining available ideas and repurposing them in a patchwork way as needed. He puts the Bricoleur in contrast to the Engineer, who tries to construct a comprehensive holistic narrative. Accordingly, he frames the Bricoleur as the "savage mind" and the Engineer as Western science. Philosopher Jacques Derrida criticizes Lévi-Strauss's distinction: "The odds are that the engineer is a myth produced by the *bricoleur*." Simply put, Derrida is arguing that the distinction between fluid, playful, improvised systems and those that seem fixed, stable, and immutable "decomposes" as soon as we acknowledge that all structures either fall somewhere in between, or that perceived stability is just another element in the Bricoleur's tool belt. Lévi-Strauss, Claude. *The Savage Mind.* Chicago: University of Chicago Press, 1966. Derrida, Jacques. *Writing and Difference.* Chicago: University of Chicago Press, 2017.

15. Freire, Paulo et al. *Education for Critical Consciousness.* New York: Continuum, 1973.

16. Some people use the term *bro-ism* simply to describe the "bro speak" euphemisms that permeate "bro culture." I use *bro-ism* in a more

grammatically formal way, adding the suffix *-ism* to turn the noun *bro* into an action (like heroism and barbarism), while also acknowledging how coded speech and mannerisms transform an informal way of expressing group solidarity into an ideological or religious system (like Judaism, liberalism, or fundamentalism).

INDEX

INDEX

in father–daughter relationship, 102,
108, 109, 113, 115–116, 125, 131,
208n5, 209n12
as type of love, 101
estradiol, 203n56
estrogen, 49, 203n56
estrogen receptors, 203n56
evolutionary psychology, 66

family patterns
critical consciousness and, 145–146
democratic organization of family life,
113, 115, 116, 118
heterosexual cohabitation and, 129–130
locker-room gender essentialism and,
103, 111–112, 163–164, 167
narcissistic patriarchal authority and,
72–73, 125
nuclear family structure, 7, 125,
126–130, 212n37
perpetuation of, 18–19, 33–34
rigorous inclusivity and, 172–173
family values, 7
father-figure identity
of adoptive fathers, 203n59
adultness and, 138
anti-sexist perspective of, 45, 64
aspirational models of, 8, 10, 31
authority and, 30, 155
colliding myths and, 117–118
divorced fathers and, 5
father–daughter relationship and, 103,
107–111, 117
gender binaries and, 130
gender essentialism and, 50–51, 105
hero's journey and, 40
inadequacy and, 152
interpretation of, 169
narcissistic patriarchal authority and,
51, 52
Oedipus complex and, 44–45, 130
father figures. *See also* feminist dads
aspirational images of, 8
assumptions about, 7–8, 177

authority of, 19, 30, 41, 43, 57–58, 65,
69–70, 72, 81, 112, 149, 177
caretaking role of, 8, 17–19, 22–23, 24,
25–28, 44, 50, 52, 127
dearth of imagery of, 32
father's voice in head, 18, 19, 176–177
habits of mind, 103
hero's journey and, 39–42
mirroring world's apathy and
indifference, 44
paternal abandonment and aggression,
43
popular images about, 7
in progress, 175–177
reinvention of, 51–52
self-intervention for, 11
Father's Day, 109
femininity
affective experiences associated with,
35, 150
characteristics culturally associated
with, 35, 49, 77–79, 81, 109–110, 136,
166–167
feminism
breast-feeding and, 26
defining of, 8–10
as framework informing actions, 10–11
matriarchal societies and, 45
second-wave feminism, 106
social and cultural analysis of, 153
feminist dads. *See also* responsive
fathering
anti-sexist perspective and, 64, 126, 136
assumptions interrogated by, 45, 60,
94–96, 140–141, 153
autonomy and, 71
avoiding ego fallacy, 62, 98
characteristics of, 8–9
cooperative intelligence and, 97
critical consciousness of, 12, 91, 97–98,
117, 141–153, 168, 177
father–daughter relationship and, 103,
116–117, 120, 122–125, 135
foundational principles of, 12–15

INDEX

feminist dads *(cont.)*
  household duties and, 127–130,
    161–164, 168
  locker-room gender essentialism
    challenged by, 103–104, 161–168,
    177
  male psychology and, 37
  maturity and, 176
  as model, 12
  motivations of, 27
  mutual subjective realities and, 90
  nuclear family and, 126–127, 130
  ongoing, iterative practice of, 10
  reinvention of father figure and, 51
  rigorous inclusivity and, 14, 168–173,
    177
feminist theory, 91
First-Daughter Effect, 121
Fliess, Wilhelm, 37
folktales
  narcissistic patriarchal authority in,
    71–72, 73, 74–82, 155
  patrilineage in, 81
Frankfurt, Harry, 205n14
Frazer, James, 23–24, 85
Freire, Paulo, 141, 144–147, 149–150,
    159–160, 170
Freud, Sigmund, 37–38, 40, 42–45, 84,
    102, 105–106, 135

gaslighting, 82–84, 88, 89, 92, 113, 155
gender
  archaic narratives of, 27
  cultural construction of, 142
  defining characteristics of, 46, 50
  renegotiation of categories of, 31
  sex distinguished from, 46–47, 50
gender binaries
  challenging of, 14, 78, 103, 202n50
  father–daughter relationship and, 111,
    123
  father-figure identity and, 130
  parenting roles and, 34
gender discrimination, 31

gender equality, 127, 132, 162–163, 167
gender essentialism. *See also* locker-room
    gender essentialism
  anti-sexist rhetoric replacing, 13
  as cultural reality, 169
  father-figure identity and, 50–51, 105
  of Jungian psychology, 50–51, 77–78,
    136
gender identity, 6–7, 52
gender inequality, 25–26, 31
gender neutrality, 10, 123
gender-nonconforming individuals, 14,
    111, 169, 202n50
gender-related political issues, 120–122
gender roles
  challenging of, 93
  in Industrial Age, 7, 34, 35–36, 37, 38,
    41, 112, 138
  parenting and, 7, 24–25, 34, 127–130,
    212n37
  sexism in origins of, 34, 200–201n34
  shifts in, 46
  specialization of, 35
gender stereotypes
  challenging of, 93–95, 132–133, 169
  father–daughter relationship and, 122,
    131–132
generation gap, 41
genital binaries, challenging of, 103, 131
Gen X, 116, 126
#GirlDad, 122, 123–124
Glynn, Adam N., 121
Goffman, Erving, 21, 114
Good Men Project, The, 128–129
Gottlieb, Lori, 204n64
gravity, 205n12
Greek mythology
  Aphrodite, 60
  Athena, 60, 110
  fatherhood in, 57–59, 155
  Hephaistos, 57–58, 204n2
  Hera, 57, 204n2
  polytheism of, 59, 61
  Zeus, 57–61, 68, 83, 110–111, 159

222

INDEX

INDEX

INDEX

INDEX

Stewart, Patrick, 69
Streeter, Edward, 209n13
subject/object dualism, 84–90
sugar hypothesis, 99–100
survival of the fittest, 66
Swanson, Barrett, 201n39
Swift, Taylor, 22
symbolic deprivation, 115, 210n23
symbolic indulgence, 115, 210n23

technological disruption, 42
testosterone, 22, 49, 50
thunderbolts
    as metaphor for determined action,
        60–61, 62, 65, 95, 116, 168
    of Zeus in Greek mythology, 58, 59,
        60–61, 159
toxic masculinity
    behaviors and attitudes associated
        with, 35, 66, 78–79, 151
    bro-ism and, 164–168, 216n16
    coded messages of, 132
    fathers enacting elements of, 43, 93
    systemic forces behind, 201n39
    transition from, 64, 150
transgender individuals, 14
transphobia, 91, 151, 153, 159, 166, 167
Tribble, Bud, 88–89
Trump, Donald, 6, 212n34
truth
    inner voice and, 70
    intersubjective and equitable truth, 97
    listening mindfully and, 170
    narcissistic patriarchal authority and,
        72, 156
    responsive fathering and, 156
Twitter, 122
tyrannical behavior, business leaders
    praised for, 65

UBS Global Wealth Management, 115
umbilical cord, fathers' cord-cutting
    ritual, 44, 159
understanding, listening distinguished
    from, 156–157, 158, 168
unmarried parents, gender of, 6–7
unreliable narrators, 53, 204n64

vagina dentata, as archetypal motif,
    133–136
Valentine, Helen, 107
Valentine's Day, 99–102
Vernant, Jean-Pierre, 41
virtue signaling, 10
von Franz, Marie-Louise, 73, 77–81
Vonnegut, Kurt, 19

Wallace, David Foster, 142, 214n2
Wall Street Journal, 3, 4
Watkins, Mary, 147
white supremacy, 12, 92, 141, 149, 167
Willingham, Emily, 66
windmills, 67, 86–87, 88
women
    assertiveness of, 109–110
    caretaking role of, 27–28, 34, 38, 44,
        127–128
    child-rearing responsibility of, 26
    empathy altruism hypothesis and,
        119–120
    father's role in sexual awakening of,
        102–105, 106, 107–110, 111,
        112–113, 115–116, 118–119, 123,
        209n13
    mother-infant bond, 25–26, 159
    patriarchal expectations of, 112
    reproductive rights of, 31–32
    testosterone in, 49
    as working mothers, 127

ABOUT THE AUTHOR

Jordan Shapiro, PhD, is father to two children and step-father to two more. He lives in Philadelphia with his partner, Amanda Steinberg. He teaches in Temple University's Intellectual Heritage Program. He's senior fellow for the Joan Ganz Cooney Center at Sesame Workshop, and nonresident fellow in the Center for Universal Education at the Brookings Institution. His previous book, *The New Childhood* (2018), received wide critical acclaim and has been published in eleven languages.

Follow him on Twitter: @jordosh
Instagram: @jordosh
Facebook: facebook.com/jordosh
Visit his website: www.jordanshapiro.org